D1710037

Grassfield Press, Miami Beach

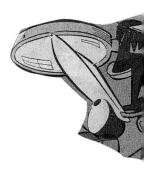

Bruce Helander:
Curious Collage

By Robert Mahoney

Introduction by Henry Geldzahler

SCHOOL OF THE MUSEUM
OF FINE ARTS — BOSTON

Grassfield Press, Inc.
P.O. Box 19-799
Miami Beach, FL 33119

Works by Bruce Helander © Bruce Helander, 1993
Pl. 10: Collection of The Art Institute of Chicago, gift of Dr. Martin A. Gecht
Introduction © Henry Geldzahler, 1993

Library of Congress Catalog Card Number: 93-080843

ISBN 0-9628514-6-9 (cloth)
ISBN 0-9628514-7-7 (paperback)

Jacket: (front) *Record Rendez-vous*, 1993
(back) composed by Bruce Helander, 1993

Title Page: Bruce Helander, *Magnifying Magpies*, 1993

End papers (cloth edition) selected and composed by Bruce Helander, 1993

This book is dedicated to the memory of

Suzanne Morgan

and her impeccable vision and taste.

1. *Wheeler Dealer*, 1969, collage, 11 x 8 in. Collection of the artist

Preface and Acknowledgments

When Grassfield Press moved its operations from Los Angeles to Miami Beach in 1990, we were eager to discover the hidden treasures of this region. During one of our excursions we had the pleasure to view a number of collages by Bruce Helander, who makes Palm Beach his home. Our response to these intimate works composed of vintage printed paper was so immediate and enthusiastic that we decided to publish them in this monograph, the first on Helander's work and career. As Helander has a special flair for design and a heightened sensitivity to printed matter, we invited him to create and select compositions especially for this book, including the back jacket, end papers (cloth edition) and the title page, *Magnifying Magpies*. It has been a unique experience and great pleasure working with Bruce Helander and we are very appreciative of all the time and care he devoted toward the publication of this book.

We would like to join the artist in thanking Robert Mahoney for his insightful and informative text; Henry Geldzahler for capturing the spirit of the artist and his work in the introduction to this book; Susan Hall and Kimberly Marrero of the Helander Gallery, Palm Beach, for the long hours they devoted to gathering photographs and information; Sue Henger for copy editing the text; Katell Besnard for the French translation; Janet Eaglstein for her assistance with the proofreading of the manuscripts; and Elaine Weber for the design of this special book. In addition, the artist would like to express his gratitude to the following individuals for their generous assistance and encouragement along the way: His mother, Carmen, and daughter, Klee; Doug and Dale Anderson; Gabrielle Brown and Neil Watson, Helander Gallery, New York; Blake Byrne; Dale Chihuly; Alan and Marcia Docter; Bill Drew; Paul Fisher; Ethan Karp; Ivan Karp; David Klein; Kenneth Kneitel; Carlo Lamagna; Mimi Livingston; Tony Longoria; Richard Merkin; Louis Mueller; Robert Nelson; Carole Newhouse; Todd Oldham; Jed Perl; Michael Price; Michael and Elizabeth Rea; T. Alec and Arlette Rigby; framers David Riggs and Bob Risley; Dan Rizzie; Selma Robinson; Dean Rosenbach, Esq.; Italo Scanga; Kenn Speiser; John Torreano; and exhibitions specialist Russell White.

James and Bonnie Clearwater
Publishers, Grassfield Press

In all his activities, Bruce Helander has the instincts of a magpie and the energy of a carnival pitchman. As an artist his great loves are the printed page and the art of illustration. His collages, whose underimages can be read as heaving landscapes or pneumatic female forms, are lovingly constructed out of pre-used printed paper that has been deconstructed and reconstructed by his instinct for the manipulation of shallow space, for the airy closure of collaged abstraction.

The breadth of reference Helander's work draws on comprehends both the magical twilight of America's Golden Age of book illustrators, Maxfield Parrish, N.C. Wyeth and Howard Pyle, and the Abstract Expressionist compositional devices of James Brooks' paintings and John Chamberlain's sculpture. It was his fascination with illustration that drew Bruce to the Rhode Island School of Design in the late sixties, confirming his earliest forays into pop culture as a boy isolated on a Midwestern farm, tracing and rubbing comic strip panels.

Bruce Helander, the magpie accumulator of printed paper in thrift shops and flea markets, is fascinated by publications as varied as Mexican soft porn, French comic strips and American mechanics magazines. He acquires them in huge drafts in Florida, New York and Paris and familiarizes himself with them on hundreds of nights seated in his studio—a glorified desk really—where he rubs and cuts and fits together scraps and images that retain their varied cultural identities in collages of amazingly civilized density.

2. Bruce Helander in his Palm Beach studio

On first viewing a Helander collage, one is likely to see snippets of anecdotal interest; the focus at first is on the origin of each "brushstroke"; as the work becomes more familiar we step back, so to speak, and the composition becomes a landscape throughout which the artist creates footpaths of entry and exit that guide and delight the eye. The documentary aspect of the work was perfectly captured in critic Jed Perl's reference, "the paled out aniline color of old-fashioned color newspaper supplements" (ironically no longer entirely old-fashioned, as once again newspapers have turned to four-color separation, bringing printer's colored ink full circle in a century).

The tradition within which Helander's works can be traced back at least as far as the Gay Nineties in Paris, to Toulouse Lautrec's lithographic posters of the cancan and the circus and to the creation of name-brand identification in advertising (wine, tobacco, travel) through poster illustration on a grand scale. More modern ways of addressing the public were devised using new technology in the effort to capture the popular imagination and the public's attention.

Our realization, tardy and conflicted, that this was done exclusively for commercial reasons explains the proliferation of categories of artistic endeavor, e.g., fine art, pop art, commercial art and kitsch, so naturally intermixed in American art since 1960, just as the rather simplistic need to limit art to its proper category has made such a hash of art and cultural criticism. Purists for whom only fine art is legitimate remain blind to the true richness and complexity of the sources of which artists avail themselves, where fine art, pop, illustration and kitsch merrily jostle each other.

Helander's work is refreshing in that it helps make sense of the information overload that assaults our sensorium at every turn. The manageable size of his collages (manageable both in the making and in the viewing) and their meticulous handmade construction serve to tether symbolically the threat to our senses and to our intelligence that technoculture produces — the words and numbers and images in which we drown. If intelligence lies in our ability to pick among the myriad signals through which we swim, as Alfred North Whitehead has written, Helander's collaged arrangements of the detritus of our century provide an antidote to overload. Never overwhelmed by his material, he turns excess to good effect and makes it work for him.

On a visit to Bruce's house in Palm Beach, we recognize the wit and humor so evident in his art. Bruce collects collections, as it were; there is rarely one of anything, and in some cases (tablecloths with maps printed on them) four hundred is more like it. Excess is the watchword. In his collecting as in his art, he is more interested in the serial than in the unique, in the manufactured than the handmade. For him, low material is precious, large and small are consistently reversed and, in every way, the classical canon is subverted.

As the same principles can be said to apply to the work as to the collecting, we come away with the conviction that the man and the artist are one, quirky and authentic.

Henry Geldzahler
Southampton, NY

Avec l'instinct d'une pie et la force d'un homme à poigné, Bruce Helander s'adresse à toutes ses activités. Son amour pour les pages imprimées et pour l'art de l'illustration se manifeste à travers toute son oeuvre artistique. Ses collages, qui naissent de la superposition d'images, représentent des paysages ou des formes féminines pneumatiques. Ils sont faits de papiers imprimés usagés qu'Helander décompose et recompose avec une maîtrise infaillible de l'espace et de fermeture aérienne de l'abstraction du collage. L'ampleur de l'inspiration d'Helander va de la magie crépusculaire de l'âge d'or des illustrateurs de livres comme Maxfield Parrish, N.C. Wyeth et Howard Pyle, au système de composition abstrait expressionniste des peintures de James Brooks et de la sculpture de John Chamberlain. Sa fascination pour l'illustration l'a conduit à Rhode Island School of Design à la fin des années 60. Il put ainsi, donner une nouvelle dimension à son approche de la culture Pop. En effet, jeune garçon isolé dans une ferme du Midwest des Etats-Unis, il traçait, et gommait des bandes dessinées. Telle une pie, Helander accumule les papiers imprimés qu'il trouve dans des boutiques d'occasion ou aux marchés aux

3. Bruce Helander's Palm Beach house

puces. Sa captivation va des publications mexicaines légèrement pornographiques, aux bandes dessinées françaises en passant par les magazines de mécanique américains. Il les achète en énormes quantités en Floride, à New York ou à Paris. Il s'en imprègne pendant les centaines d'heures, où, assis dans son atelier - en fait un bureau du plus bel aspect - il frotte, coupe, réunit, gratte les images qui plus tard conféreront aux collages leur identité multiculturelle d'une densité incroyablement riche. Lorsque l'on regarde un collage d'Helander pour la première fois, on verra à coup sûr, des morceaux de papier d'un intérêt anecdotique. En premier lieu, on se concentre sur l'origine de chaque «coup de pinceau», puis, en se familiarisant avec le collage, on prend, pour ainsi dire, du recul et la composition devient un paysage à travers lequel l'artiste crée des entrées et des sorties pour guider et satisfaire le regard. L'aspect documentaire de l'oeuvre de Bruce a été parfaitement saisi dans la critique de Jed Perl «la couleur analine passée des suppléments couleur de journaux démodés» (ils ne sont ironiquement plus démodés puisqu'en utilisant à nouveau la quadrichromie, on ferme la boucle d'un siècle d'utilisation de la couleur). Helander s'inspire de sources aussi lointaines que le gai Paris des années 1890, les lithographies de Toulouse Lautrec sur le Cancan et le Cirque, et le début de la fabrication en grand nombre d'affiches publicitaires représentant des marques de vin, de tabac, de voyages. L'utilisation de nouvelles technologie a permis l'imagination des moyens plus modernes d'attirer l'attention du public et de captiver l'imagination populaire. La prise de conscience tardive et discordante du but exclusivement commercial de ces technologies explique que a prolifération d'activités artistiques dans les beaux-arts, l'art Pop, l'art commercial et le kitsch et donne matière à la critique culturelle. Et ceci, juste au moment où le besoin plutôt simpliste de limiter l'art à sa propre catégorie se fit sentir.

4. Bruce Helander's Palm Beach house

Les puristes ne légitimisent souvent que les beaux-arts et sont aveugles à la véritable richesse et à la complexité des sources dont les artistes savent profiter et d'où les beaux-arts l'art Pop, l'illustration et le kitsch qui se bousculent et se mélangent joyeusement. 🐦 L'oeuvre d'Helander est réconfortante dans la mesure où elle nous aide à donner un sens à toutes les informations qui agressent notre sensibilité. La petite taille des collages - maniables: lors de leur création et dans la manière de les voir - et leur construction méticuleuse contribuent à attacher symboliquement la menace qu'exerce la techno-culture (les mots, les chiffres et les images qui nous submergent) envers nos sens et notre intelligence. Nous nageons dans une myriade de signaux, et si, comme l'a écrit Alfred North Whitehead, l'intelligence repose sur notre habileté à les choisir, Helander nous procure, avec ses collages composés des détritus de notre temps, l'antidote à la surcharge. Il n'est jamais débordé par l'excès de matériaux. Au contraire, il le tourne à son avantage en lui donnant le meilleur effet. 🐦 Dans sa maison de Palm Beach, on discerne l'esprit et l'humour dont il fait preuve dans son art. Helander collectionne; chez lui, on trouve rarement un seul objet d'une même catégorie mais plutôt dans certains cas - comme les nappes imprimées de cartes - quatre cents spécimens. L'excès est le mot d'ordre. Dans ses collections, comme dans son art, il s'intéresse plus à la série qu'à l'unique, au manufacturé qu'au «fait à la main». Pour lui, le matériel sans valeur est précieux, le petit et le grand sont inversés et le canon classique est, de toute façon, subverti. 🐦 Dans le mesure où les mêmes principes peuvent être appliqués à son oeuvre artistique et à ses collections, on peut conclure avec conviction que l'homme et l'artiste sont unis — singuliers et authentiques.

Henry Geldzahler
Southampton, NY

5. *Curtain Call* (diptych), 1969, collage, 10 x 8 in. Collection of the artist

Bruce Helander was born in 1947, in the middle of the Baby Boom, and grew up in the middle of the United States, in Great Bend, Kansas, and Racine, Minnesota. His mother, Carmen was a dancer and singer of Spanish descent who had attended the Rhode Island School of Design in the years just before World War II. His father, Amos, was a handsome man of Swedish stock known for his outlandish style of dress and eccentric tastes, including a large collection of hand-painted ties. Both of these creative persons encouraged their son's artistic impulses.

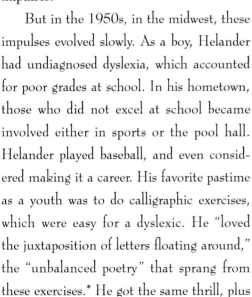

6. Bruce Helander, age 3, Great Bend, KS

But in the 1950s, in the midwest, these impulses evolved slowly. As a boy, Helander had undiagnosed dyslexia, which accounted for poor grades at school. In his hometown, those who did not excel at school became involved either in sports or the pool hall. Helander played baseball, and even considered making it a career. His favorite pastime as a youth was to do calligraphic exercises, which were easy for a dyslexic. He "loved the juxtaposition of letters floating around," the "unbalanced poetry" that sprang from these exercises.* He got the same thrill, plus

"a pat on the back," in helping his father paint the signs for the family's grocery store. He discovered that design was the only place where it was acceptable for him to employ the twists and turns of letters he saw in his mind. His impulse to create collages emerged from the pleasure he experienced in "inventing shapes, twisting things around, and adding spice to something that already existed." For a young boy who was a failure academically, art was the one area in which he could excel and gain the admiration of his family and peers.

When Helander was thirteen, his father died. His mother remarried in 1963, and the family moved to Minnesota. Helander responded to the disruption in his life by collecting and hoarding found objects. "I would collect old rusted cans and bring them to my window sill: My stepfather must have thought I was off my rocker." Helander also collected fountain pens, advertising labels, bowling shirts and restaurant menus. For Helander, collecting unusual objects became a private act of protecting his individuality. During his

*All quotes by the artist are from interviews with the author, May and July 1993.

teen years, he also experimented with transferring images from comics and the front page of the *Minneapolis Star*. He would apply lighter fluid to the newsprint and rub it against a sheet of paper until the image appeared. (Despite the similarity of technique to Robert Rauschenberg's transfer drawings of the 1960s, the young Helander was oblivious to modern and contemporary art.)

It was during Helander's troubled teen years that he realized "there was something going on creatively" within him. He came to the conclusion that the only way

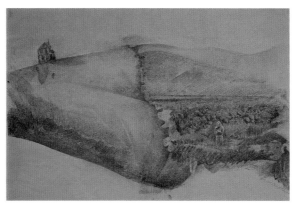

7. *Mother Earth*, 1965, lighter fluid transfer with pencil, 18 x 12 in.
Collection of the artist

to release this creativity was to seek professional guidance and training in art outside of the midwest. "It was do or die for me to get into a place like the Rhode Island School of Design," he later recalled. Perhaps influenced by his mother, an alumna, Helander passed up several midwest art schools to pursue his studies at RISD, the oldest and most traditional college of art in America.

Helander's arrival at RISD in 1965 coincided with its heyday. From 1965 to 1975 competition to get into RISD was fierce and the quality of students was

unusually high. A number of RISD graduates contributed to the general swing away from the prevailing modernist values to a sensibility that by 1974 was called postmodernism. Like other artists of his generation, Helander moved away from the modernist emphasis on pure form, color and flat picture plane. Matisse, who was an influence on the minimalists' quest for pure color and form, inspired the succeeding generation's exploration of decoration and new materials. First-generation feminist work by artists such as Miriam Schapiro and Joyce Kozloff sparked interest in feminine culture materials and handwork, such as quilting, tapestry making and sewing. The decorative aesthetic injected itself into the abstractionist mainstream and brought forth Pattern and Decoration painting. "Decorative," "humane," and "organic" were the words in the air.

Around this time, the painter Richard Merkin and the assemblagist Italo Scanga had become RISD's young maverick instructors. Merkin, a sophisticated bon vivant from New York, "was a real style maker." For Helander, sitting in Merkin's class was like attending a performance. Merkin would come into the classroom in eccentric outfits that he had had custom made or that he had found in the second-hand stores of Providence. He used a vintage pointer and flourished a Hollywood-style attendance book. Merkin thus impressed on his students that "you don't stop being an artist when you leave the studio — even when you address an envelope." In his own work, Merkin incorporated old postcards and bits and pieces of letters and paper as assemblage elements on canvas. Merkin opened Helander's eyes for the first time to the aesthetic of adaptive reuse and to the witty redemption of objects that "already had a spirit to them." Merkin even influenced the way Helander dressed (echoing Helander's father's own stylish influence). In order to savor the aura of the secondhand, Merkin was known to commission a new suit and leave it hanging in his closet for a few years until it got the right hang to it.

Scanga, in some ways, was similar to Merkin, and in others he was his opposite. An Italian immigrant with a "natural instinct" for cooking and a flair for arranging objects and collecting, Scanga grasped at life with a meaty fervor. Scanga also believed in being a "twenty-four hour artist" and impressed on the young Helander that "everything you find or see will come back to your work." It was Scanga who began to

bring Helander and his best friends among RISD students, Dale Chihuly, Bill Drew and Kenn Speiser, every Sunday to their "own religious ceremony": The Norton, Massachusetts flea market. Chihuly, who always rose at four in the morning and was at work on drawings for new glass pieces by five, had no trouble with the early morning necessity of getting to the flea market before the good stuff was gone. Helander, until then a late riser, learned this discipline from Chihuly's and Scanga's example. Chihuly scoured the markets for all types of glass, especially green kitchen glass. He also picked up folk art and outsider art. Helander focused on old paper — stationery, envelopes, posters — that had a sense of a past deeper than his own. "As I came from the midwest where there was no vintage anything, I was attracted to unusual and odd antiques and vintage paper," notes Helander. Scanga concentrated on utilitarian objects that had a certain "aroma" of use or oddness that he could incorporate into a sculpture. He challenged himself in trying to appreciate bereft found objects and resurrect them into his sculptural medium. Scanga amazed his students by the catholic scope of his interests, often buying whole cardboard boxes of castoff objects and junk in which he found some relation and use for his art.

Helander ranged outside the fine art department as well, considering various career options. He took an elective course in the graphic design department from Sewell Sillman, a teacher and printer known for completing with Norman Ives at Yale University *The Interaction of Color*. Sillman had studied under Joseph Albers at Black Mountain College in the late 1950s. During his time at RISD, he was working on a second book project investigating Albers' color theory. Sillman's course on color theory was demanding and severe. He taught Helander about the subtle gradations of color that appear at an edge and the way dimension and colors change when different colored pieces of paper touch. Sillman noted, as well, how a series of gradations in a single color could result in a concave or louvered appearance at the edge. The impact of these lessons is evident in Helander's approach to color in his collages.

In the graphic design department, Helander also met Malcolm Grear, a well-known designer who created graphics for New York's Solomon R. Guggenheim Museum. Grear introduced Helander to the decorative use of graphic symbols and letter forms. In exercises relating letter forms to human figures or juxtaposing letters and fine art symbols, Helander recaptured the spirit of his boyhood calligraphy drills. The department also provided Helander the opportunity to link his love of paper to photography by studying with Harry Callahan and Aaron Siskind, whose photographs

have the appearance of abstract paintings or collage work.

The RISD scene, outside the classroom, stirred up interaction between the arts. Experimental music was central to this scene. Martin Mull, a good friend of Helander's at RISD and later a successful actor and painter, started a band called Soup with conceptual/performance artist Neke Carson. Charles Clavery (who later joined the television cast of "Saturday Night Live") founded Young Adults, which, to Helander was the first great "art rock" band, combining aesthetics of fashion, music, lyrics and outrageous behavior in a kind of highbrow dada performance art fused with rock music. Helander also started a band (as the drummer), working his way through three years at RISD. In the RISD scene, Helander remembers, "music could be anything you wanted it to be." Andy Warhol "loved RISD" and visited frequently with the Velvet Underground, presenting a series of performances that had a profound impact on the scene. David Byrne was briefly at RISD, in 1972, before quitting to form with two other RISD students the sophisticated art rock group Talking Heads. During the same period, the great jazz saxophonist Scott Hamilton emerged from the RISD community. "Making art with music was easy," Helander notes, "the quickest way for a sophisticated intellect to express ideas." The collage of musical

16

inventiveness was thus a "creative arm" of Helander's academic experience.

Activities both in and out of the classroom created an atmosphere for a certain style at RISD. The most interesting work being produced involved mixing folk, popular and design materials with a high art edge. Dale Chihuly accomplished this with glass, David Byrne with music, and Nicole Miller with fashion. Later, Jenny Holzer, a graduate student in 1974, would bring language into art in a new way with her own biting angle. Jedd Garret, who was at RISD in 1970, also epitomized the RISD style of

8. Bruce Helander in sunglasses with his band, Black River Circus

narrative eccentricity, a sophisticated, highbrow cultivation of the "left-footed nuttiness" of found objects, images and words. Mary Boone, another ambitious classmate, utilized her instincts and experiences at RISD to forge her gallery in New York's SoHo.

In this atmosphere, Helander came to adopt collage as his art form. Although his graduate show included a large painting with objects attached to it [pl. 63], by the second year of the graduate program he was working exclusively in collage. He often went into the school's museum and studied the paintings and paper cutouts of Matisse and the collages of Kurt Schwitters. Collage allowed Helander to cultivate paper as a material in its own right, much as Chihuly did with glass. He also saw collage as a visual equivalent to jazz, allowing him the same dada-surrealist craziness as epitomized by the collages of Max Ernst. And he compared the "second or third layer" of collage — the use of bits of cartoon and overheard conversation — to the jump cuts in film editing.

Helander's education, then, was exemplary of the RISD style: A material-based collagist aesthetic. While each artist focused on one new material, the dimension of that focus was enriched by constantly looking over the shoulder at other arts. Some artists change styles radically after graduating from art school, but the artists of RISD's heyday generally discovered their forte in the 1970s and stayed the course.

Helander became involved in all aspects of the arts at RISD. As a graduate student he worked in the admissions office. Six years later, at the age of 29, he was offered the position of provost (dean of the college) and charged with the day-to-day functioning of the college. During his tenure from

1979 to 1981, he arranged for honorary degrees to be offered artists like Rauschenberg and Betty Parsons. In 1981, his restless entrepreneurial energy led him to resign from RISD to start *Art Express*, a magazine that covered the national art scene. In 1982 he sold *Art Express* to *Horizon* magazine and with the proceeds of that sale moved to Palm Beach, Florida, and opened the Helander Gallery. (He opened a gallery in New York in 1989 and continues to shuttle between his two spaces.) Dealing art forced Helander to speak extemporaneously on creativity all day, every day, sharpening his focus and enriching his taste. Helander benefited from the relocation of important contemporary artists to Florida as well, and acted as Florida dealer for John Chamberlain, Duane Hanson, Kenneth Noland, Jules Olitski, Larry Poons, Rauschenberg and James Rosenquist. He also remained committed to showing promising younger artists and presented exhibitions of old RISD associates Bill Drew, Louis Mueller and Martin Mull. Ironically, he also became the New York dealer for his former teachers, Richard Merkin and Italo Scanga.

All of this frenetic daytime activity on behalf of other artists' work channeled Helander's own creative energies into stolen hours in evening studio sessions. "Collage is an extension of the limitations that I have as a very engaged person in the profession,"

Helander commented. Collage, Helander's chosen medium, is an intimate art form that can be done in a small space, for a few hours at night with the door shut against the world. This routine fell into place at RISD. In Florida, Helander found the ability to work longer uninterrupted hours in his studio every night.

Bruce Helander has learned to explore every element of the limited formula available for developing collage: shapes, color harmonies, depth and texture. Beyond these basic principles, Helander combines the iconographic elements of his resource material to create delicate psychological connections — oppositions and irony, humor and wit.

Most of the collages consist of roughly a dozen torn pieces of paper lifted from old magazines, ads, song sheets, maps, comics and wallpaper. In works comprising materials from a single source (old magazines, for example), the composition has a flat consistency and muted tone, while works made up of various contrasting sources of paper have an open and jumpy appearance.

In single-source works, Helander tends to emphasize the mending of fragmented pieces of paper by sanding down the paper, a technique he learned from painter/teacher Bill Drew. Sanding creates several effects: First, it flattens the paper and accentuates the lines so that there is a consistency in the integration of shapes. Second, it allows the eye to glide on color rhymes and jump over the more abrupt iconographic juxtapositions. This keeps the eye from reading the collage elements too fast, in effect holding the abstract note a bit longer. Finally, sanding often brings up ghost images from underlayers of the source paper, lending a palimpsest richness and phantom romance to these collages. Under the sanded surface, iconographic elements "become a kind of camouflage within the whole composition." In these works, it appears that color is making the form and controlling the tone of the work. When Helander

9. *Atlantic Avenue*, 1991, collage, 20 x 5½ in.
Collection of Wendy Cohen, New York, NY

uses two flush pieces from the same source, he orients halves of an image in reverse position: One body part points left, the other, turned upside down, points right. This juxtaposition usually occurs in the center of the collage, setting off a slight whirlpool effect, as in *Record Rendez-vous* [pl. 30] and *Buster Blue* [pl. 20]. Folding the central image in on itself results in a contemplative mood, an appealing ennui, a melancholy and fateful tone.

Helander's cultivation of an aged patina enriches the melancholy tone of these works. It is primarily the patina of his materials and the small scale of his works that create an intimacy for the viewer that is fundamental to the nature of collage. "A collage, for me, cannot be successful if it is larger than fifteen or twenty inches in any direction," Helander insists. In this respect Helander reinforces Meyer Schapiro's theory that collage must have derived from still-life depiction, as it conveys "man's sense of control over his material life." ** The visual tiptoeing that takes place within Helander's intimate scale allows the eye to roll off the sanded edges of the paper elements and pursue and exult in the smallest idiosyncracies of the material and subject without upsetting the composition as a whole.

**Meyer Schapiro, "The Apples of Cezanne: An Essay on the Meaning of Still-life" (1968), *Modern Art. 19th and 20th Centuries: Selected Papers* (New York: George Braziller), p. 19.

In works where several paper sources are used, the torn or cut pieces of paper seem to bump with a thud against each other. In most of his collages, Helander lays down a foreground object in such a way that everything behind it falls into an illusion of depth and perspective. To amplify this illusion, Helander often provides a fantasy horizon, a mountain range, treetops, or an aerial view (always in the top half of the picture) as a way out of the jumbled maze. Color clashes and bright jazzy tones are also characteristic of the multiple-source works. Reverse orientation of images at the center, swirling composition and three-dimensional coloration serve to lead the eye toward the iconographic "jump cut" effect. *Atlantic Avenue* [pl. 9] and *Jungle Jazz* [pl. 58] are examples of this jumpier hemisphere of Helander's creativity.

After Helander completes his composition, he rubber stamps it with the date of its execution. The date stamp, like Helander's signature, is incorporated into the design of the collage. A date stamp is traditionally an image of vintage consciousness and ties in with Helander's proclivity to collect. Library stamps on old books and date stamps on collectible issues of out-of-print magazines are part of the administrative iconography of collecting paper. By incorporating a date stamp into the collage, Helander puts a seal of time on the work. But he also tricks the eye. Expecting to see a date that coincides

with the age of the collage element (early twentieth century), one is surprised upon seeing the date of the work's execution (late twentieth century). (In the same manner, Helander tucks away his own signature within the composition so that it is not immediately recognizable, in effect sanding down the role of the author.) The stamped date therefore establishes the collage's existence in time as part of an ongoing series of collages. Each piece is as much a graphic record of the time taken to make it as of the thought processes that went into its creation. That is, it represents a moment in time when Helander "collected himself" in a work of art.

Helander's work ultimately is about collecting. His choice of titles for his collages is also an extension of his collecting activity. Each title consists of two words beginning with the same letter: *Baby Blues, Earning Everyday, Stage Set*, etc. The serial-style titles relate to the collecting aesthetic, for as Helander learned from the Philadelphia artist and collector of objects, Harry Anderson, one pair of salt and pepper shakers is nice, but only rows and rows of sets of them can be beautiful and amount to art.

Helander's own collection of objects overlaps with his art. He collects tramp art, twig chairs from the 1950s, folk art carvings, "bad" or thrift shop paintings, salt and pepper shakers (400 pairs), wooden soap dispensers, tourist map tablecloths from the

1940s and 1950s, teapots, ashtrays, vintage photographs, eccentric lamps, and advertising props from the 1940s (featuring the Esquire Man, the Porter Paint Man, the Delta Battery Man). Helander's vintage paper collection, consisting of thousands of sheets of papers and posters, forms the physical bridge between his collecting and his art making. His home (itself one of the oldest houses in Palm Beach, a turn-of-the-century cottage) enshrines these endless collections, all arranged in rows on shelves, counters, bureaus and tables. His home environment has much in common with his art studio. All the details of his living environment are occupied by his collections, lending a pleasant "collage environment of surprise, humor, romance and pure re-discovery of the human impulse to create" to every aspect of his domestic life. In other words, Helander lives in another of his collages.

The period from which most of Helander's collections date coincides with the period of most of the source material for his collages. He notes with longing that the 1920s, 1930s and early 1940s was a period in which objects were manufactured with an aesthetic sensitivity and a love of craftsmanship that have since been lost. In printing, especially, those years were marked by extraordinary care and craftsmanship. He saves paper from this period in his collection and at the same time redeems it in

his art. Scouring the flea markets, he searches for good specimens for his collection and preys on irreparably damaged specimens for his art. At times he defers using a beautiful piece of paper that he intuitively knows will work well in the art, storing it in a cigar box for that rainy day when he at last feels ready to use it. Collecting and collaging, then, are not just physically linked for Helander, they are joined by siamese-twin connections that elicit complex and heart-wrenching decisions about their use.

Although most of Helander's source material dates from the 1920s and 1930s, he is attracted specifically to some of the quirkier aspects of that age. For instance, he prefers the 1930s song sheets in a stylistic transition between art nouveau and art deco. His images often represent the Jazz Age, but from an exoticized French perspective, the same orientation that encompassed the "orientalist" eccentricities of Josephine Baker. His images of soft porn are culled from Mexican publications in which the mores of the times demanded that nude bodies be "dressed" in classical poses. Their thinly veiled pretense gives the work an "unsophisticated yet graphic kookiness" that Helander admires. (His admiration, while not quite camp delectation, is in fact a recognition of the "funny" or "bad" datedness of the poses.) These offbeat sources offer Helander a vocabulary of means for outsmarting the limited formula of collage. He transcends the monotony of arranging pretty pieces of paper by throwing ironic curveballs and sliders. The qualities of dumbness or silliness challenge the viewer by spinning off multiple possible interpretations. They build humor into the work and create achingly sweet or acute psychological effects that might be blocked by more straightforward material. Thus Helander creates a roller coaster ride of visual interest in his work.

Each source material has its own inherent spirit and a specific form that seems to influence (perhaps unconsciously) how Helander alters it. Looking at these different caches of material, one can identify certain iconographic categories of Helander's work: Erotica, Dreams, Cartoons, Eccentric Landscapes, Painterly Effects and Meanders.

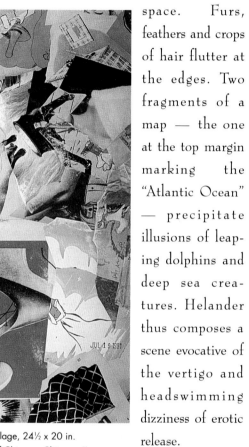

10. *Spiral Stare*, 1991, collage, 24½ x 20 in.
Collection of The Art Institute of Chicago, Chicago, IL

EROTICA

The facture of collage seems to lend itself naturally to abstract depictions of the ecstatic moments of erotic feeling. Helander infuses his erotic collages with both the ecstasy and the complications of sex. In *Atlantic Avenue* [pl. 9] a female figure is cut up and turned in on herself. Multiple fragments of body curves rotate around a blank space. Furs, feathers and crops of hair flutter at the edges. Two fragments of a map — the one at the top margin marking the "Atlantic Ocean" — precipitate illusions of leaping dolphins and deep sea creatures. Helander thus composes a scene evocative of the vertigo and headswimming dizziness of erotic release.

Flower Fire [pl. 25] presents a pinup girl in a tragicomic way. The clichéd tease pose of head turned over bare shoulder dominates the center of the collage. The contorted figure twists into a cigarette butt rubbed out by the shoespin of a debonair dancer circling around the model. The mood of the dancer alternates: At times he is effaced, at other times he lifts a cane against the pinup, and, still, at other times he almost licks her feet. Neither an appeasing bouquet of flowers below nor a ball gown poised like an exclamation point at the top (a symbol of respectable female attire) can shake the leonine eroticism out of the blind and faceless femme fatale.

In *Fish Fancy* [pl. 21] a fresh coquette at center has turned into a one-eyed mermaid with the fish at the wrong end. She tries to clean herself with cleanser sprinkled from a can on the right, but she continues to radiate an aura of sexuality. Visions of dresses and

11. *Devil's Dream*, 1993, collage, 16¾ x 13¼ in.
Collection of Elizabeth and Michael Rea

pearls fill up her bath, carrying her along in a joyous toilette preparing for love. But a word fragment, "eaning," in the upper left-hand corner, mixes EAting with cleaNING to undercut her joy with the fear that she will be devoured by the goldfish.

Record Rendez-vous [pl. 30] is erotic insofar as it incorporates a fault line along

the breast of a "sweater girl." Perhaps her sweater quakes with memories of boys pressing against girls during slow dancing in the dark. But her left arm, enlarged by the fracture of the paper, warns of the whack that will ward off suitors who try to get too familiar. A calliope-style quartet of singing soldiers pipes up to sing "[y]ou beautiful doll" to the spiral-headed sweater girl. They have ogled her and admired her beauty but never pressed against her.

In *Spiral Stare* [pl. 10] Helander incorporates Mexican soft porn images from the 1930s by transforming a figure in a dramatic pose from "modern dance" (which made nudity artily acceptable) into a seductive earth-mother figure. The nude's reaching gesture is enriched by the jumble of surrounding images: The Big Bad Wolf (an extension of the nude's left hand) falling into the fire, a ruffled vanity table, a spiral staircase and an overall trashing of house and home. In *Devil's Dream* [pl. 11] Helander cut up a

23

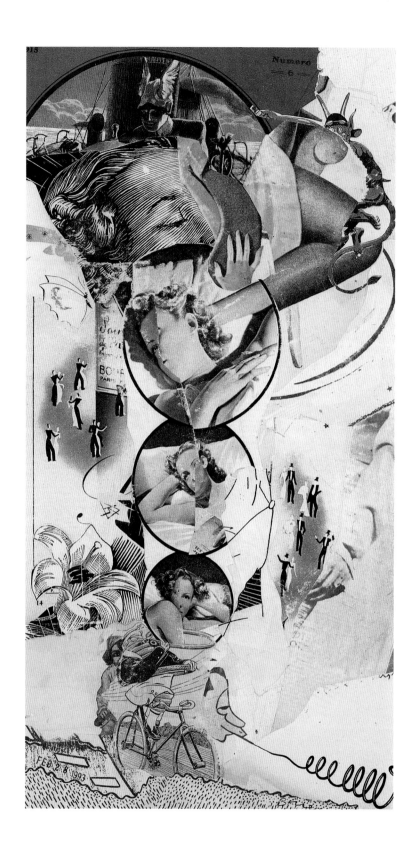

12. *Bubble Balloon*, 1993, collage, 15 x 8 in. Courtesy of Arij Gasiunasen Fine Art, Palm Beach, FL

photography scrapbook from the 1930s that demonstrated how to light nudes in the dark and reassembled the figures to form the face of a devil. In all of Helander's erotic collages, ranging from the sad to the comic (such as the satirical *Double Dip* [pl. 27]), the complications and roller-coaster energy of the erotic life is played to the extreme.

D R E A M S

Several of Helander's collages inadvertently recapture dreams or express content in such a way that they can be interpreted as dreams. Headlessness, or substituting something else for the head, usually on a female muse figure, often signifies entry into a dream state. In *Headless Housewife* [pl. 22]

13. *Earning Everyday*, 1991, collage, 20 x 15½ in.
Collection of the Philadelphia Museum of Art, Philadelphia, PA

a half-dressed figure supported by one leg hops into a land where even the breastlike huts echo her nudity. The nightmare of appearing naked before a crowd takes on geographical dimensions. This basket-headed woman replays an ordeal of the past in which housewives dreamed of public life but awoke in a cold sweat, trembling at their exposure. Peripheral images suggest other themes: A tiny man with a brush paints and perfects a woman's face as a reenactment of *Pygmalion*. Behind the breadbasket head is a silhouette of a hatted man sharpening a scythe. One motif discusses life and art, the other life and death.

Wonder World [pl. 33] finds a cartoon globehead pushed into bed in his red striped pajamas by a tall, diplomatic ghost with a stylish hood over his face. This World of Counterpane is beset with dishbreaking maids and bobbed-hair visitors from the social whirl. All the while, the bed seems to unravel like ribbons as the hand of a femme fatale rocks the cradle into an abyss.

Three effaced figures rest their heads on pillows in the middle of *Bubble Balloon* [pl. 12]. Here, too, the reveries of sleepiness bring up images of "I could have danced all night." Boutonnieres frame the image from below. But as the eye runs up this emotional thermometer, the mercury (and a ship's Mercury figurehead crowns the totem pole) in the poses gets agitated. A raised arm breaks out of the circle into a twist of devil's tails, grasping hands and a seductive leg. Finally, a face recedes like a sunset into the orange glow of a seafaring scene, which illustrates but a work of fiction. The reveries of pillow talk thus feed back into themselves without regard for reality.

In *Torino Tornado* [pl. 23] a ripped-open tire tread, highlighted by an image of Atlas prying open the world, exposes mermaid fantasies beset by little red

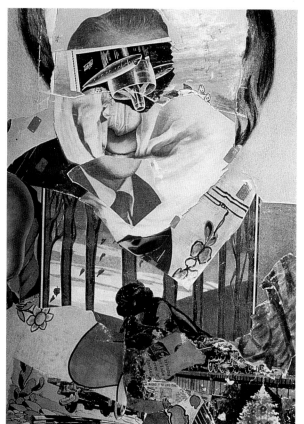

14. *Dave's Delirium*, 1991, collage, 15 x 10½ in.
Collection of David Zimmerman, New York, NY

devils. The collage seems to say: A man must break his back to earn his day of leisure. But, here, too, the thrill of swimming turns quickly into the fear of drowning. Like all of Helander's dream collages, this one starts with the sleepiness of the

muse and ends with a nightmare that snaps it awake.

CARTOONS

Helander uses cartoon elements in almost all of his collages to add comic spice to the iconographic level of meaning. In some collages the presence of these figures is prominent enough to sway the tone toward popular imagery without actually becoming Pop Art. Unlike Warhol and Roy Lichtenstein, Helander gears his interest in popular culture toward the eccentric and personal content found in the small motifs — "the second or third layer of meaning." These secret meanings infer a private joke or a sophisticated game that separates Helander's works from Pop's embrace of mass culture conventions and cliches. Still, when Helander leans toward Pop, cartoons tend to dominate.

Earning Everyday [pl. 13] is Helander's

most outright comic collage, a parable of getting and spending that rides the gamut from cartoon pratfalls on rockslides to a western desert peak neatly framed by that ultimate sign of blow-smoke-in-your-face humiliation—the single smoke ring. A strange cat presides over the various stunts.

Helander's use of cartoons keeps his grim comment on the futility and ridiculousness of consumerism within the comic vision of life. In other collages Helander emphasizes the cartoon characters' ability to rebound from danger, disasters and even death, adding pluck, drive, farce and esprit to the darker side of human nature.

15. *Stage Set*, 1991, collage, 15½ x 11½ in.
Collection of Louis and Wendie Helander, Temecula, CA

ECCENTRIC LANDSCAPES

As Helander makes use of map fragments and meteorological references, it is inevitable that several collages become veritable landscapes. *Dave's Delirium* [pl. 14] is moored in the land by a stand of fairy-tale trees spread across the collage. This enchanted forest becomes the site of an unresolved family drama in which a kneeling hooded figure is caught in an impasse of sputtering jump starts between thoughts of going home for the holidays (a locomotive runs over a Christmas tree in the lower right corner) and equally strong thoughts of running away. Over this scene looms a father figure which Helander has fused with science fiction hardware.

In *Stage Set* [pl. 15] old Coney Island's City of Light amusement park evokes memories of America the Beautiful. Other landmarks of cottages and fertile fields fill out the idyll. George Washington crosses the Delaware only to end up in California. There, a 1940s country-western band makes the window curtains dance. It is a happy history, bought for a song.

Mighty Mississip [pl. 18] turns a quaint sip of water into a broad flood of dreams.

16. *Chef's Charade*, 1993, collage, 15 x 10½ in. Courtesy of Virginia Lynch Gallery, Tiverton, RI

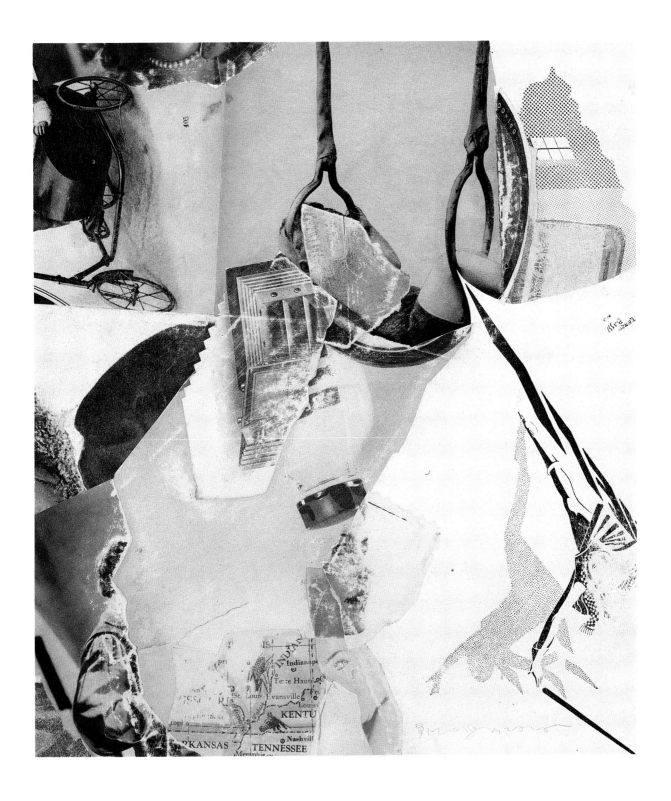

17. *Bike Barrage*, 1993, collage, 11¼ x 8½ in. Collection of Senator and Mrs. Howard Metzenbaum, Washington, DC

Freight is neatly boxed on preindustrial docks, where the labor is easy. The tall fish stories of idle men are represented in a small fishing vignette upper left. A woman perched on top of the mountains suggests that it's a woman's world. In all of Helander's eccentric landscapes a picaresque spirit retells the legends of travelers and explorers as they continue to enrich the escapist dimension of the American dream.

PAINTERLY EFFECTS

Some of Helander's collages are almost entirely abstract. They feature as their main iconographic elements, bursts of steam or smoke, the illustrative evocations of the thrown, the spread, the flounced, the

18. *Mighty Mississip*, 1991, collage, 9¼ x 10 in.
Private Collection, Los Angeles, CA

dripped. These works illustrate collage's lineal descent from painting. Such pieces seem all aflutter and in constant motion. *Chef's Charade* [pl. 16] is typical of these graphically kinetic works. A hand reaches for a stack of pancakes, an arm emerges from a Shirley Temple dress, a foot steps on a sewer, forks fly, surgical instruments amass. In almost every case, the pursuit of iconographic meaning is cut off by the pure ener-

gy of the depicted movement.

In *Bike Barrage* [pl. 17], another abstract piece, there is indeed a bulky side-wheel bike in the upper corner, but it is too closely associated with a pearl necklace to suggest speed. Exercise rings extend downward from top center, but their grip is obscured. The exaggerated leap of a dancing figure at the right is hardly discernable. Disembodied faces, sanded down by the artist, are all agog at the dancer's incredible movement. The mapped confluence of the Ohio and Mississippi rivers suggests the effort of two souls (or legs) to come together, but only the wheeling, the swinging and the leaping come through. An abstract totem of racing thoughts remains.

In all the works in this category, iconographic elements are subordinated to their capacity, by illustration, to describe the relationship between the act of placing a collage element and the action of painting a brushstroke.

MEANDERS

Helander lets loose with purely abstract scrolls of pattern and decoration in some of his collages. These are dominated by a linear effect, with lines meandering every which way, never allowing the viewer a rest. *Analytical Advice* [pl. 57] features a cubistic jumble of black-and-white line drawings wiggling in all directions. *Boogy Buff* [pl. 19] uses a map from which to launch lines on contradictory paths. The "boogy" is a reference to Mondrian's paintings, but the meandering lines contradict Mondrian's geometric grid. In *Jungle Jazz* [pl. 58], one of Helander's most abstract collages, letters and red ribbons trace out a *chanson*. The French Tricolor adds a frenetic energy to the curls of red ribbons. At the center is the ultimate icon of crazy meandering, a chicken running around without its head.

Bruce Helander's collages look back to a past that was symbolized by Gatsby's green light and the Emerald City of Oz. Made from materials imbued with the golden age of printing, the collages are both nostalgic and redemptive. They tour the shadows, throw curve balls and put an ironic and comic spin on life. Yet, like the best of decorative art, they always return to an irrepressible joy of living, expressed in their movement and color. With this joy comes hope, a rare emotion in the late twentieth century, but one which allows Bruce Helander to recreate America as the promised land.

Robert Mahoney

19. *Boogy Buff*, 1991, collage, 8 x 6 in. Collection of T. Alec and Arlette Rigby, Manalapan, FL

Bruce Helander naquit en 1947 en plein «baby boom». Il grandit dans le centre des Etats-Unis, à Great Bend au Kansas puis à Racine dans le Minnesota. Espagnole de souche, sa mère, Carmen, était chanteuse et danseuse. Elle fut étudiante à Rhode Island School of Design (RISD) pendant les années précédant la seconde guerre mondiale. Amos, son père, bel homme d'origine suédoise était renommé pour son style vestimentaire et pour son goût pour les excentricités, comme par exemple sa collection de cravates peintes à la main. C'est dans ce milieu créatif que Bruce Helander développa ses dispositions artistiques. Dans le Midwest américain des années 30 elles ne pouvaient croître que lentement. Enfant, Bruce Helander souffrait de dyslexie et ses résultats scolaires s'en ressentaient. Or, dans sa ville natale ceux qui n'excellaient pas dans leurs études s'adonnaient au sport ou au billard. Helander choisit le base-ball. Il pensa même devenir professionnel. Adolescent, il se passionna pour les exercices calligraphiques, faciles à réaliser pour une personne dyslexique. Il «adorait la juxtaposition des lettres qui flottaient», la «poésie déséquilibrée» qui «bondissait» de ces exercices.* En aidant son père à peindre l'enseigne de l'épicerie familiale, il ressentit la même émotion, le même frisson. C'est alors qu'il comprit que le dessin était le seul moyen agréable de mettre à profit les tours et détours qu'il imaginait. Son désir de réaliser des collages vint du plaisir qu'il éprouvait en «inventant des formes, en entortillant des choses et en ajoutant quelque chose à quelque chose qui existait déjà». Pour un jeune garçon médiocre à l'école, l'art était le moyen d'exceller et d'obtenir l'admiration de sa famille et de ses amis. A 13 ans, Helander perdit son père. Sa mère se remaria en 1963 et la famille déménagea dans le Minnesota. A la suite de cette rupture, il se mit à collectionner et à amasser les objets qu'il trouvait. «Je collectionnais les vieilles boîtes de conserve rouillées que je mettais sur le rebord de ma fenêtre, mon beau-père devait penser que j'étais un peu loufoque». Helander collectionnait aussi les stylos plume, les étiquettes publicitaires, les chemises de bowling et les menus. Pour lui, collectionner des objets insolites devenait une façon secrète de protéger son individualité. Durant son adolescence, il fit des expériences en transférant des images de bandes dessinées et des couvertures du «Minneapolis Star». Il appliquait un liquide plus clair sur le papier journal puis frottait la page contre une feuille de papier jusqu'à ce que l'image apparaisse (ignorant tout des courants de l'art moderne ou contemporain, sa technique présentait pourtant des similitudes avec celle des transferts de Robert Rauschenberg des années 60). Pendant les années troublées de son adolescence Helander réalisa qu'il «se passait quelque chose de créatif» en lui. Il en conclu que s'il voulait libérer son énergie créatrice, il devait quitter le Midwest pour aller se placer sous l'égide de Professeurs. «Pour moi, intégrer une école comme RISD était une question de vie ou de mort». C'est sans doute parce que sa mère avait étudié à Rhode Island School of Design, la plus vieille et la plus traditionnelle école d'art des Etats-Unis, qu'il négligea les écoles d'art du Midwest pour l'imiter. En 1965, lorsque Bruce arrive à Rhode Island School of Design, l'école jouissait d'une excellente réputation. De 1965 à 1975, la compétition pour y rentrer était féroce et les étudiants étaient particulièrement doués. De nombreux diplômés de cette école participèrent à la tendance générale, en se tournant vers une nouvelle sensibilité qu'en 1974 on appela postmodernisme. A l'instar de ces artistes, Bruce Helander s'éloigna des valeurs modernistes dont l'accent portait sur l'applat, la forme et la couleur pures. Matisse influença les minimalistes dans cette même quête et inspira la génération suivante dans sa recherche de l'utilisation d'éléments de décoration et de nouveaux matériaux. Miriam Schapiro et Joyce Kozloff furent à l'origine des premières oeuvres féministes et déclenchèrent un vif intérêt pour les matériaux employés dans les travaux féminins comme le patchwork, la tapisserie et la couture. En somme, l'esthétique décorative s'était introduite naturellement dans la tradition abstraite, grâce à l'utilisation de motifs et de la peinture décorative. Les mots en vogue étaient alors : «décorative», «humaine» et «organique». Le peintre Richard Merkin et «l'assembleur» Italo Scanga, jeunes diplômés, sont les nouveaux professeurs «non conformistes» de Rhode Island School of Design. New Yorkais sophistiqué, Merkin est un bon vivant, «un vrai faiseur de style». Helander assiste aux cours de Richard Merkin comme on va au spectacle. Merkin arrivait en cours vêtu d'ensembles excentriques qu'il faisait tailler ou qu'il dénichait dans des friperies de PROVIDENCE. Il utilisait une vieille baguette et se servait d'un cahier de présence aux fioritures hollywoodiennes. Il démontrait ainsi à ses élèves qu' «ils ne cessent d'être artiste lorsqu'ils quittent l'atelier... pas même lorsqu'ils rédigent une enveloppe». Dans son oeuvre personnelle, il utilisait de vieilles cartes postales, des bribes de lettres et des morceaux de papier qu'il incorporait comme éléments à part entière dans la composition de la toile. C'est Merkin qui ouvrit les yeux d'Helander sur l'esthétique qu'offre la réutilisation adaptive, et sur la rédemption spirituelle des objets qui possèdent «déjà un esprit». C'est encore Merkin qui influença les goûts vestimentaires d'Helander (se faisant ainsi l'écho de l'influence paternelle). Enfin, Merkin était connu pour se faire confectionner des costumes qu'il laissait se patiner dans son armoire jusqu'à ce qu'ils obtiennent un fini parfait, et ce, afin de jouir pleinement de l'aura du Temps. Italo Scanga ressemblait par certains côtés à Richard Merkin, mais pouvait parfois lui être totalement opposé. Scanga, immigré Italien, avait un «instinct naturel» pour la cuisine, un flair pour disposer et collectionner les objets. Il saisissait la vie avec une ferveur acharnée et pensait lui aussi que l'on est artiste «24 heures sur 24». Il apprit au jeune Helander que «chaque chose que l'on voit revient un jour dans son art». Tous les dimanches Scanga emmenait Bruce et ses meilleurs amis de RISD (Dale Chihuly, Bill Drew et Kenn Speiser) à leur «propre cérémonie religieuse»: le marché aux Puces de Norton au Massachusetts. Dale Chihuly se levait toujours à quatre heures du matin et commençait à travailler vers cinq heures sur les dessins de ses nouvelles pièces de verre ; il n'avait donc aucune difficulté à se rendre au marché aux puces avant que toutes les bonnes affaires ne soient parties. Helander,

20. *Buster Blue*, 1993, collage, 10 x 6¼ in. Private Collection, Miami Beach, FL

au contraire, avait l'habitude de se lever tard, mais en suivant l'exemple d'Italo Scanga et de Dale Chihuly il apprit à se discipliner. Chihuly écumait les marchés à la recherche de plusieurs sortes de verres et plus particulièrement les verres de cuisine de couleur verte. Il achetait aussi des objets folkloriques et même «ringards». Les recherches d'Helander se concentraient sur les vieux papiers, la papeterie, les enveloppes, les affiches (ces objets possédaient un passé plus profond que le sien) : «comme je venais du Midwest où il n'y avait aucune antiquité, j'étais attiré par les vieux objets inhabituels, disparates et les papiers d'époque». Italo Scanga quant à lui, cherchait des objets utilitaires qui se distinguaient par leur «arôme» singulier. Plus tard, il se lançait un défi: ressusciter et donner une âme à ces objets trouvés, par le biais de la sculpture. 🐎 Les préoccupations catholiques d'Italo Scanga étonnaient ses élèves. Il achetait souvent des cartons entiers d'objets sans valeur et de bric-à-brac afin servir de son art. 🐎 Helander se situait en marge du département des beaux-arts et ne savait toujours pas quelle direction donner à sa carrière. Il s'inscrit au cours de dessin graphique de Sewell Sillman, un professeur et imprimeur connu pour avoir écrit avec Norman Ives à l'Université de Yale *The Interaction of Color*; Sillman avait eu Joseph Albers comme professeur à l'Université de Black Mountain à la fin des années 50. A l'époque où il enseignait à RISD, Sillman travaillait sur un second projet de livre ayant pour sujet la théorie de Joseph Albers sur la couleur. Sillman était un professeur exigeant et sévère. Ses cours sur la théorie de la couleur, enseignèrent à Helander la maîtrise des graduations subtiles des couleurs et lui apprirent à jouer sur la dimension et les couleurs grâce à la disposition des morceaux de papier entre eux. Scanga lui montra comment une série de dégradés de même couleur pouvait donner une apparence concave aux rebords. 🐎 C'est dans ce département de l'Université qu'Helander rencontra Malcom Grear. C'était un célèbre dessinateur, auteur du graphisme du musée «Solomon R. Guggenheim» de New York. Il initia Helander à l'utilisation graphique des symboles et des lettres. Ce dernier devait mettre en relation des lettres avec des corps humains ou juxtaposer des lettres avec des symboles des beaux arts. Il y redécouvrit, l'esprit des exercices calligraphiques de son adolescence. Les cours d'Harry Callahan et d'Aaron Siskind lui ont également donné l'opportunité de lier son amour du papier à la photographie. 🐎 A RISD, après les cours, une interaction s'établissait entre les différentes disciplines. La musique expérimentale était au centre de la scène. Le célèbre acteur et peintre Martin Mull, qui était un bon ami d'Helander à RISD, forma avec Neke Carson (un artiste conceptuel) le groupe «Soup». Charles Clavery, qui plus tard fit partie de l'équipe de l'émission télévisée «Saturday Night Live» forma le groupe «Young Adults». C'était, d'après Bruce Helander, le premier grand groupe de «rock art». Il alliait l'esthétique de la mode à celle de la musique, du lyrisme et de la poésie. Leur comportement sur scène était outrageant, leur style un mélange d'art «Dadaiste intellectuel» et de musique rock. Helander monta un groupe (il y était batteur) qui eut du succès pendant trois ans. Il se souvient qu'à RISD «la musique pouvait être tout ce que vous vouliez qu'elle soit». Andy Warhol «adorait RISD»; il venait souvent avec le «Velvet Underground» pour donner des représentations qui marquèrent profondément les étudiants de l'école. En 1972, David Byrne fit un bref passage à RISD avant de former le groupe de rock art «Talking Heads» avec deux autres anciens élèves de l'école. A la même époque, le grand saxophoniste de jazz Scott Hamilton se distingua de la communauté de RISD. Helander découvrit que c'était facile de faire de l'art avec de la musique: «pour un intellectuel sophistiqué, c'est la meilleure manière d'exprimer ses idées». ✑ L'influence de la création musicale fut donc une «arme créative» dans l'expérience académique d'Helander. ✑ Toutes ces activités scolaires et extra-scolaires de RISD produisaient une ambiance qui conduisait les élèves à adopter un certain style. Une bonne oeuvre d'art devait comprendre un mélange essentiel d'éléments folkloriques, populaires et de dessin de haute qualité. Chihuly appliquait ce principe au verre, David Byrne à la musique et Nicole Miller à la mode. Plus tard, Jenny Holzer (diplômée en 1974) apporta au langage artistique une nouvelle dimension avec ses formules personnelles caustiques. Jedd Garret qui était à RISD en 1970, employa lui aussi le style narratif excentrique spécifique de RISD. Ce style se singularisait par l'utilisation sophistiquée et intellectuelle de la «douce folie» des objets trouvés, des images et des mots. Mary Boone, une autre ambitieuse camarade de promotion mit à profit ses dispositions naturelles et ses études à RISD pour monter, plus tard l'une des plus importantes galeries de SoHo (New York). ✑ C'est dans cette ambiance qu' Helander décida que le collage serait la forme d'art à laquelle il se consacrerait. A l'occasion de l'exposition de fin de première année, il présenta une grande peinture d'où pendaient des objets. Mais dès sa seconde année d'études, il se consacra exclusivement aux collages. Il se rendait souvent au musée de l'école où il étudiait les peintures et les collages de Matisse et de Kurt Schwitters. Les collages permettaient à Helander d'utiliser le papier comme une matière à part entière, un peu comme Chihuly le faisait avec le verre. Il les considérait aussi comme l'équivalent pictural du jazz. Ils permettaient d'exprimer «une folie dada-suréaliste» semblable à celle qu'offraient les collages de Max Ernst. Il comparait aussi «la deuxième et la troisième» couche du collage «là ou il utilise des bribes de bandes dessinées, et de conversations» aux chutes des montages de films. ✑ RISD offrait une formation tres caractéristique et Helander était un bon représentant de ce style, qui reposait sur l'utilisation esthétique de la matière dans le collage. A l'époque, la préoccupation de tous les artistes était la recherche d'une nouvelle utilisation de la matière. Pour ce faire, ils ne cessaient d'examiner toutes les autres formes d'art. Ce regard aitique apportait une plus grande intensité à leur réflexion. Une fois diplômés, certains artistes de RISD changeaient de style, mais les étudiants qui trouvèrent leur style à la grande époque de l'école, dans les années 70, y restèrent fidèles. ✑ Helander s'impliqua dans tous les aspects de la vie artistique de RISD. Il travailla au bureau des admissions. Six ans plus tard, à 29 ans, on lui proposa le poste de Principal et il fut chargé du fonctionnement quotidien de toute l'école; il conservera cette fonction de 1979 à 1981. Au cours de cette période, il remit des diplômes honorifiques à des artistes comme Robert Rauschenberg et Betty Parsons.

En 1981, sa fébrile énergie d'entreprendre le poussa à démissionner de RISD pour monter le magazine *Art Express*, qui couvrait la scène artistique nationale. En 1982, il le céda au magazine *Horizon* et, grâce au bénéfice de sa vente, il déménagea à Palm Beach où il ouvrit la galerie Helander (il en ouvrit une autre à New York en 1989 et continue aujourd'hui encore ses allées et venues entre les deux galeries). Sa fonction de marchand d'art, oblige Helander à parler continuellement de créativité, il a ainsi aiguisé sa passion et perfectionné son goût. Helander a su tirer partie de l'arrivée d'importants artistes contemporains en Floride et est devenu le marchand de John Chamberlain, Duane Hanson, Kenneth Noland, Jules Olitski, Larry Poons, Rauschenberg et James Rosenquist. Il continue néanmoins à s'occuper de jeunes artistes prometteurs et organise des expositions pour d'anciens camarades de RISD comme Bill Drew, Louis Mueller et Martin Mull. L'ironie du sort l'a aussi amené à devenir le marchand New Yorkais de deux de ses anciens professeurs de RISD, Richard Merkin et Italo Scanga. 🐿 Les activités frénétiques qu'il exerce pour les autres artistes contraignent Helander à n'utiliser sa propre énergie créatrice que pendant les rares heures où, le soir il s'enferme dans son atelier pour faire ses collages. Ils sont «le prolongement des limitations imposées à une personne très engagée dans son métier». Ce faisant, il a choisi une forme d'art très intimiste à laquelle il peut s'adonner, à l'écart du monde, dans un petit espace durant quelques heures, chaque nuit. Cette habitude lui vient de RISD. Helander a trouvé en Floride la possibilité de travailler chaque nuit dans son atelier pendant de longues heures sans être interrompu.

🐿 Bruce Helander a appris à explorer chaque élément du procédé limité dont il dispose pour fabriquer un collage; il joue sur les formes des fragments de papier, l'harmonie des couleurs, la profondeur et la matière. Au delà de ces principes de base, il faut explorer les éléments iconographiques de la matière qu'il utilise de façon créative. Helander utilise des connexions psychiques délicates (opposition et ironie, humour et esprit) afin d'étayer la consistance de son oeuvre. 🐿 Dans la plupart de ses collages, Helander utilise à peu près une douzaine de morceaux de papiers tordus qu'il trouve dans de vieux magazines, des publicités, des partitions de musique, des cartes, des bandes dessinées et des papiers muraux. Dans certaines de ses oeuvres, les composantes proviennent d'une source unique (vieux magazines par exemple); la composition a alors une constance plate et une tonalité sourde. Au contraire, les collages composés de papiers de provenances diverses, donnent une impression d'ouverture et offrent une cadence saccadée. 🐿 Dans les oeuvres «mono-source», Helander a tendance à accentuer le côté «raccommodage» des pièces fragmentées en ponçant le papier: cette technique lui vient du peintre et professeur Bill Drew. Le ponçage crée plusieurs effets. Tout d'abord, le papier aplati accentue les lignes, procurant ainsi une constance dans l'intégration des formes. Ensuite, il oblige l'oeil à glisser sur les rimes de couleur et à sauter vers les juxtapositions iconographiques plus abruptes. Ceci empêche le spectateur

21. *Fish Fancy*, 1993, collage, 9 x 12 in. Courtesy of Jeanine Cox Fine Art, Miami Beach, FL

de lire les différents éléments du collage trop rapidement, et maintient la note abstraite un peu plus longtemps. Enfin, le ponçage fait souvent apparaître les images «fantômes» des couches inférieures procurant ainsi une richesse palimpseste et un romantisme fantastique aux collages. Sous la surface poncée, les éléments iconographiques «deviennent une sorte de camouflage dans toute la composition». Dans ces oeuvres, la couleur fait la forme et contrôle l'esprit du travail. Lorsque Helander coupe une image en deux, il oriente les deux moitiés dans deux directions opposées: une partie regarde vers la gauche, et l'autre, retournée à l'envers regarde vers la droite. En général, ce genre de juxtapositions se situent au milieu du collage et créent un léger effet de tourbillon, comme par exemple dans *Record Rendez-vous* [pl. 30] et *Buster Blue* [pl. 20]. L'image centrale repliée sur elle-même produit plusieurs effets: elle conduit à un état d'esprit contemplatif, confère un sentiment d'ennui et donne un accent de fatale mélancolie. Cet accent est intensifié par la patine sur laquelle Helander insiste. C'est essentiellement la patine des matériaux et la petite taille des oeuvres qui procurent un sentiment d'intimité lorsque l'on regarde un collage. Pour Helander, ce sentiment d'intimité est fondamental à la nature des collages «pour moi, un collage ne peut être réussi que si sa taille n'excède pas 40 x 50 cm». A cet égard, Helander rejoint la théorie de Meyer Schapiro selon laquelle les collages doivent s'inspirer des natures mortes qui procurent «à l'homme un sentiment de contrôle sur la vie matérielle».** La petite taille des collages oblige l'oeil à se déplacer lentement. L'oeil s'éloigne de la bordure des éléments poncés pour poursuivre sa course et la terminer dans les plus petites idiosyncrasies: le sens de la composition comme un tout n'est jamais perturbé. Dans les collages où il utilise des morceaux de papier de provenances diverses, les fragments de papier tordus ou coupés semblent s'entrechoquer sourdement les uns contre les autres. Dans la plupart de ces collages, Helander applique un objet en premier plan. Ceci procure une illusion de profondeur et de perspective aux éléments situés en arrière plan. Il amplifie ce phénomène en composant souvent des paysages imaginaires. Les chaînes de montagne, les cimes d'arbres ou les vues aériennes (toujours dans la moitié supérieure du collage) nous offrent un chemin pour sortir du labyrinthe. Les couleurs qui explosent, les tons qui éclatent sont aussi caractéristiques du style d'Helander. Les images renversées qu'il insère au milieu du collage, la composition tourbillonnante et le caractère tridimensionnel des couleurs oblige l'oeil à sauter vers les variations imprévisibles de l'iconographie. *Atlantic Avenue* [pl. 9] et *Jungle Jazz* [pl. 58] sont les collages qui représentent le mieux les aspects les plus «bondissants» de la créativité d'Helander. Helander tamponne la date d'exécution sur ses collages. Ce tampon, comme sa signature, deviennent partie intégrante du collage. Le tampon dateur est par tradition le signe d'appartenance à une époque. Il faut donc y voir un lien avec le goût d'Helander pour les collections. En effet, les collectionneurs considèrent les dates tamponnées sur les vieux livres de bibliothèques et les dates des anciens magazines comme l'iconographie administrative des vieux papiers. La date au tampon ainsi incorporée dans le collage de Bruce Helander scelle ce dernier dans le temps. C'est aussi un clin d'oeil farceur qu'il nous fait. On s'attend à trouver une date du début du 20ème siècle qui correspondrait à l'âge des papiers utilisés pour la composition du collage, mais la date qui apparaît est en fait très proche de la nôtre. Le tampon et la signature d'Helander disparaissent dans les plis du papier, il faut du temps pour les reconnaître, ce qui place le rôle de l'auteur légèrement en retrait. La date tamponnée témoigne de l'existence du collage et lui donne une place dans le temps, affirmant sa place dans l'oeuvre jamais achevée d'Helander. Chaque composante est une mémoire graphique du temps et de la réflexion nécessaire à l'artiste pour la création d'un collage. ☞ De plus, elles sont le témoignage de l'instant de la découverte précédant l'insertion dans sa collection. ☞ La présence du tampon rappelle au spectateur que finalement, dans l'oeuvre d'Helander, tout est lié à la Collection. Même le choix des titres est en rapport avec l'activité du collectionneur. Dans chaque titre on retrouve la même lettre au début des deux mots: *Station Stop, Earning Everyday, Stage Set,* etc... ce genre est typique de la valeur esthétique des collectionneurs. Harry Anderson, originaire de Philadelphie, a enseigné à Helander qu'il est bon de collectionner un poivrier avec sa salière mais, qu'en collectionner des étagères entières était beau et conférait à l'art. ☞ La collection d'Helander empiète sur son art. Il collectionne des chaises en paille des années 50, des gravures d'art folklorique, de «mauvaises» peintures ou des peintures de boutiques d'occasion main, des salières et poivrières (400 paires), des distributeurs de savon en bois, des nappes imprimées de cartes touristiques des années 40 et 50, des théières, des cendriers, des photographies d'époque, d'étranges lampes, de truc publicitaire des années 40. Sa collection de papiers d'époque comprend des milliers de feuilles de papier, d'affiches et fait le lien entre le collectionneur et l'artiste. Sa maison, l'une des plus vieilles de Palm Beach, (un cottage de l'entre deux siècles) met en valeur toutes ces collections sans fin, disposées en rang sur les étagères, les commodes et les tables. L'intérieur de sa maison est presque une réplique de son atelier. Son environnement domestique est empli par ses collections et le fait ressembler par tous ses aspects à un collage plein «de surprises, d'humour et de romantisme qui rappellent sans cesse le besoin que l'homme a de créer». En résumé, Helander vit dans l'un de ses collages. ☞ La plupart des éléments qu'il utilise pour ses collages appartiennent à la même époque que les objets qu'il collectionne. Il remarque avec une pointe de nostalgie que dans les années 20, 30 et au début des années 40, on fabriquait des objets esthétiques, avec l'amour des choses bien faites. La fabrication de ces objets de qualité n'a malheureusement plus cours depuis longtemps. A l'époque, on excellait plus particulièrement dans le secteur de l'imprimerie. Helander collectionne d'ailleurs les papiers de cette époque et les revalorise en les transformant en collages. Il écume les marchés aux puces à la recherche d'échantillons représentatifs de cette époque et essaie d'obtenir les spécimens abîmés dont il se sert pour faire ses collages. Parfois, son intuition lui dicte de conserver bien précieusement un beau morceau de papier. Il le range dans une boîte à cigare et attend le jour pluvieux où enfin, il se sentira prêt à l'utiliser. ☞ Pour Helander, collectionner et faire des collages sont intimement liés. Il doit décider de la meilleure utilisation de chaque papier et ces choix l'amènent parfois à prendre des décisions difficiles; il est confronté à des dilemmes qui lui brisent le coeur. La plupart des papiers qu'il emploie datent des années 20 et des années 30. Il est surtout attiré par les fioritures spécifiques de cette époque. Dans les années 30, par exemple, les partitions de musique avaient un style transitoire qui se situe entre l'art nouveau et l'art déco. Ses images viennent souvent directement de l'âge du jazz. Toutefois, elles possèdent un côté exotique français de la même lignée que les excentricités «orientalistes» de Joséphine Baker. Celles qui sont légèrement pornographiques proviennent de publications mexicaines dans lesquelles les nus doivent être «habillés» grâce à des poses classiques. Leur affectation légèrement voilée donne au collage «l'aspect saugrenu sophistiqué mais malgré tout graphique» cher à Helander (son admiration n'est quand même pas la marque d'une délectation, elle vient du fait qu'il sait apprécier dans ces poses démodées le côté «drôle» et «méchant»). Les provenances originales de ces papiers offrent de nombreuses ressources lui permettant de dépasser la formule limitée du collage. Il peut ainsi transcender la monotonie de la disposition de jolis morceaux de papiers en y jetant des courbes et des glissades ironiques. On trouve dans ses collages, de éléments au caractère un peu sot ou niais qui défient le spectateur en lui offrant le tournoiement des multiples interprétations possibles. Grâce à ces qualités, le collage se remplit d'humour, et provoque chez celui qui le regarde de vives réactions psychologiques qui peuvent être agréablement douloureuses. On ne pourrait éprouver de telles sensations si les composantes utilisées par Bruce Helander étaient plus traditionnelles.   Ainsi donc, les oeuvres d'Helander entraînent l'oeil sur de véritables montagnes russes.   Toutes les sources dont les morceaux de papier proviennent possèdent un esprit inhérent et une forme spécifique qui semblent influencer Helander (peut-être inconsciemment) dans sa façon de les utiliser. Un examen minutieux permet d'identifier certains thèmes iconographiques chers à Helander: l'érotisme, les effets de peinture, les rêves, les bandes dessinées, les paysages excentriques, les méandres.

L'EROTISME

La facture du collage semble se prêter d'elle-même à la description abstraite des moments d'ivresse que procurent les sentiments érotiques. Les collages érotiques d'Helander nous communiquent, à la fois le sentiment d'extase que procure le sexe et les complications qu'il entraîne. Dans *Atlantic Avenue* [pl. 9], une silhouette féminine découpée est repliée sur elle-même. De nombreuses courbes provenant de fragments de corps pivotent autour d'elle dans l'espace vide qui l'entoure. Des fourrures, des plumes et des cheveux flottent au bord du collage. Deux fragments de carte, dont l'une indique: «Atlantic Ocean» sur la marge supérieure, accentuent l'illusion que les dauphins et les créatures de mer bondissent. Dans cette scène Bruce Helander évoque ainsi le vertige étourdissant de l'érotisme.   *Flower Fire* [pl. 25] représente une pin-up dans un genre tragico comique. Sa tête, qui regarde par dessus une épaule nue domine le centre du collage. La silhouette contorsionnée se vrille pour se terminer en un mégot de ciga-

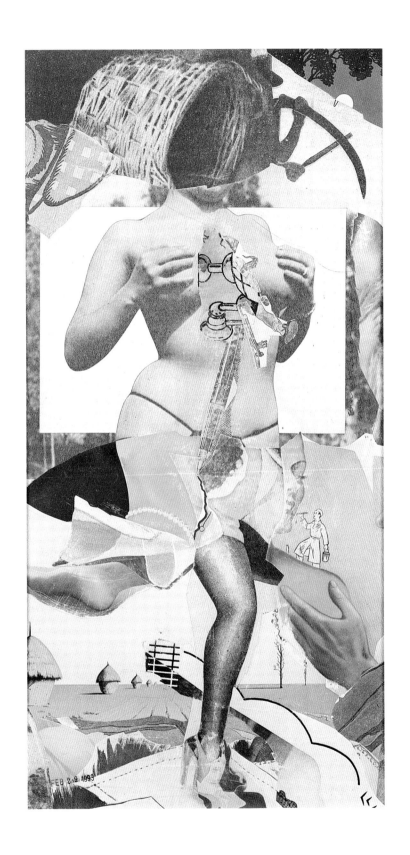

22. *Headless Housewife*, 1992, collage, 18 x 9 in. Private Collection, Chicago, IL

rette mis en retrait par la chaussure d'un danseur débonnaire. Il danse en rond autour du modèle et son attitude envers la pin-up varie. Il est parfois effacé, de temps à autre il lève sa canne vers elle, et parfois encore il lui lèche presque les pieds. Rien ne peut retirer à la femme fatale, aveugle et sans visage l'aspect érotique animal: ni le caractère apaisant du bouquet de fleurs que l'on aperçoit au bas du collage, ni la robe de bal (pourtant un vêtement symbolique de la femme respectable) qui tient en équilibre comme un point d'exclamation en haut du collage n'y parviennent. ✎ Au centre de *Fish Fancy* [pl. 21] une jeune femme coquette et ravissante se transforme en une sirène borgne dont la queue de poisson est positionnée du mauvais côté. Elle essaie de se laver en s'aspergeant d'un détergeant qui sort d'une boîte de conserve située à droite du collage, mais elle continue à dégager une aura sexuelle. Elle a des visions de robes et de perles qui confèrent un caractère joyeux à la toilette qu'elle fait en prévision de l'amour. Mais deux bribes de mots découpés: laver et manger, (en haut à l'extrême gauche), se mélangent pour gâcher sa joie en lui rappelant sa peur d'être dévorée par le poisson rouge. ✎ Le caractère érotique de *Record Rendez-vous* [pl. 30] vient de la ligne qui passe sur la poitrine de «une fille au tricot». Son tricot frémit peut-être encore du souvenir des garçons qui se sont pressés contre elle en dansant des slows durant la nuit. Mais les prétendants sont avertis, son bras gauche, élargi par un fragment de papier les écartera d'une claque s'ils prennent trop de privautés. Un quatuor de soldats évoquant Calliope se mettent à chanter «[y]ou beautiful doll» à la fille. Ils lui font les yeux doux mais n'essaient jamais de s'approcher trop près de cette fille à la tête en forme de spirale. ✎ Dans *Spiral Stare* [pl. 10] Helander insère des images des années 30 aux connotations légèrement pornographiques. Elles viennent de ses magazines mexicains. Il change la pose de la silhouette. De pose dramatique de «danse moderne» (rendant le nu acceptable), elle devient aguichante. Une foule d'images entourent la silhouette: un grand méchant loup (au bout de la main gauche du nu) tombant dans le feu, une table recouverte de dentelles, un escalier en spirale, et, tout un tas de déchets domestiques. Ces éléments contribuent à mettre en valeur la gestuelle du nu (qui regarde vers le haut). ✎ Dans *Devil's Dream* [pl. 11] Helander se sert d'un album de photos des années 30 montrant les différentes façon d'éclairer un nu le soir. Il découpe des silhouettes et les recompose en une tête de diable. ✎ Dans tous les collages érotiques, tristes ou comiques (comme la satire de *Double Dip* [pl. 27], Helander insiste à l'extrême sur les complications et la force délirante de la vie érotique.

LES REVES

✎ C'est parfois par étourderie que Bruce Helander dépeint des rêves mais parfois c'est par la manière dont le collage est exprimé que l'on peut l'interprèter comme tel. ✎ En général, la présence de la silhouette féminine d'une muse sans tête, ou à tête en forme d'objet signifie que l'on est entré dans le monde des rêves. Dans *Headless Housewife* [pl. 22] une silhouette à moitié nue erre sur une jambe dans un pays où les cases en forme de sein font écho à sa nudité. Le cauchemar d'apparaître nue devant une foule prend ici une dimension géographique. La femme à la tête en forme de panier revit la véritable épreuve des femmes d'autrefois qui rêvaient d'une vie publique mais se réveillaient en nage à l'idée d'y être exposées. Les images périphériques évoquent d'autres thèmes: un petit homme frêle parfait en peinture le visage d'une femme, remettant ainsi en vigueur la loi de Pygmalion. Derrière la tête en forme de panier à pain un homme effrayant est en train d'aiguiser sa faux. L'un des motifs parle de la vie et d'art alors que l'autre traite de la vie et de la mort. ✺ Dans *Wonder World* [pl. 33] un grand fantôme diplomatique au visage recouvert d'un crochet stylisé pousse dans un lit un personnage de bande dessinée à la tête en forme de globe qui est vêtu d'un pyjama à rayures rouges. Ce monde de courtepointe est assailli par des servantes qui cassent les plats et par des visiteurs coiffés à la Jeanne d'Arc issus de toutes les catégories du melting pot social. Pendant ce temps, le lit semble s'effilocher comme des rubans, tandis qu'une femme fatale pose la main sur un berceau placé dans une abysse. ✺ Au milieu de *Bubble Balloon* [pl. 12] trois personnages effacés ont la tête posée sur des oreillers. Ici aussi, les rêveries semblent vouloir dire «J'aurais pu danser toute la nuit» En bas, des boutonnières soulignent le collage. Mais, lorsque le regard remonte, le mercure (le haut du vaisseau Mercury couronne le haut du totem) du thermomètre émotionnel, s'agite. Un bras se lève et sort du cercle pour finir sa course dans un tournoiement de queues de diable, de mains s'apprêtant à le saisir et d'une jambe séduisante. Enfin, un visage s'éteint, tel un coucher de soleil orangé sur une scène de safari, et illustre la fiction du collage. Les oreillers et leurs rêveries se retournent sur eux-mêmes sans aucune considération pour le monde réel. ✺ Dans *Torino Tornado* [pl. 23] un pneu déchiré, mis en valeur par la présence de l'image d'Atlas priant le monde, roule, laissant des petits diables rouges assaillir des sirènes imaginaires. Le collage semble nous dire que l'homme doit se briser au travail pour mériter sa journée de loisir. Mais l'excitation de la baignade se transforme bientôt en peur de se noyer. ✺ Comme tous les collages de la série des rêves, le collage commence par l'assoupissement de la muse et finit par le cauchemar qui la réveille en sursaut.

LES BANDES DESSINEES

✺ Bruce Helander utilise des bribes de bandes dessinées dans presque tous ses collages. Il ajoute ainsi un piment comique à l'iconographie. ✺ Dans certains collages, la présence des personnages de bandes dessinées prend suffisamment d'importance pour faire balancer le ton du collage vers le Pop, sans pourtant l'assimiler complètement au Pop Art. Contrairement à Warhol ou à Lichtenstein, son intérêt pour la culture populaire vient du caractère personnel des petits motifs («c'est la deuxième ou troisième couche de la signification»). Ces significations secrètes induisent des blagues privées et un jeu sophistiqué. Elles différencient ainsi les collages d'Helander des oeuvres du Pop art qui elles, embrassaient les conventions et les clichés de la culture de masse. Cependant, lorsque les collages se rapprochent du Pop art, les bandes dessinées ont tendance à être un élément dominateur. ✺ *Earning Everyday* [pl. 13] est une parabole du processus: gagner et dépenser. C'est le collage le plus complètement comique. Il fait glisser toute la gamme des fragments de bandes dessinées sur les pentes rocheuses du mont d'un désert de western. Le mont est nettement entouré d'un rond de fumée: «la bouffée de fumée que vous recevez dans le visage». Un chat étrange préside ces voltiges. Bruce Helander trouve la société de consommation futile et ridicule, il utilise les bandes dessinées en guise de pied-de-nez et montre ainsi sa vision comique de la vie. 🐭 Dans d'autres collages, il met l'accent sur la facilité qu'ont les caractères de bandes dessinées de bondir hors du danger, de se sortir de situations désastreuses et même de la mort. Ils ont du cran, et le côté farceur de leurs aventures ne manque pas d'esprit. L'aspect le plus noir de la nature humaine s'en trouve ainsi embelli.

LES PAYSAGES EXCENTRIQUES

🐭 Bruce Helander utilise des fragments de cartes et de références météorologiques, il n'est donc pas étonnant que certains de ses collages deviennent de véritables paysages. Une fôret d'arbres de contes de fées s'étale à travers le collage *Dave's Delirium.* [pl. 14] Un drame familial insoluble se déroule dans cette forêt enchantée. La silhouette encapuchonnée d'une fillette agenouillée est surprise en pleine réflexion, elle est confrontée au dilemme suivant: doit-elle rentrer à la maison pour les fêtes? (en bas, dans le coin droit, une locomotive fonce vers un arbre de Noël) ou doit-elle s'enfuir très loin? La silhouette d'un père apparaît indistinctement dans cette scène, elle se mélange à des éléments de science-fiction. 🐭 *Stage Set* [pl. 15] est une commémoration de la ville de lumière qu'était Coney Island. Le collage fait allusion au parc d'attractions au temps de la «Belle Amérique». Des petites maison de campagne de cette belle époque et des champs fertiles remplissent ce paysage idyllique. Georges Washington traverse le Delaware et arrive en Californie. Là, un groupe de musique «country» des années 40 fait danser un rideau. C'est une histoire gaie achetée pour une chanson. 🐭 Dans *Mighty Mississip* [pl. 18] une étrange petite gorgée se transforme en une inondation de rêves. Une cargaison de caisses attendant d'être chargées est entassée sur des quais de l'époque pré-industrielle. On peut y voir la commémoration du travail facile de cette époque. Une vignette représentant un pêcheur (en haut à gauche) fait référence aux «fameuses» histoires de pêche des hommes oisifs. La silhouette féminine perchée en haut d'une montagne, suggère que c'est un monde de femmes. 🐭 A travers ces paysages excentriques Helander nous raconte les légendes des voyageurs et des explorateurs, elles contribuent à enrichir la dimension de l'évasion du rêve américain.

LES EFFETS DE PEINTURE

🐭 Certains collages d'Helander sont presque complètement abstraits. On y trouve des volutes de fumée et de vapeur, des évocations définissant les rebuts, des éléments qui s'étalent ou s'élancent, de l'eau qui tombe; le tout caractérisant les principaux thèmes iconographiques. L'oeuvre d'Helander démontre que le collage descend bien de la peinture. Tous les éléments semblent virevolter et être en perpétuel mouvement. 🐭 *Chef's Charade* [pl. 16] est typique de ces collages au graphisme cinétique. On y voit une main qui essaie d'atteindre une pile de crêpes, un bras qui émerge d'une robe de Shirley Temple, un pied posé sur un égout, des fourchettes qui volent, des amas d'instruments chirurgicaux. On est sans cesse détourné de la recherche du sens iconographique par l'énergie pure qui se dégage du mouvement. 🖎 *Bike Barrage* [pl. 17] est un autre collage abstrait. Dans le coin du haut on trouve une imposante bicyclette, mais son association avec un collier de perles placé à proximité empêche de donner une impression de vitesse. A droite, la silhouette d'un danseur effectuant un saut exagéré est à peine discernable. L'incroyable pirouette du danseur semble mettre en transe les figures désemboîtées et poncées par l'artiste. Sur un morceau de carte, on peut voir le confluent de l'Ohio et du Mississippi. Il évoque l'effort que doivent faire deux âmes (ou deux jambes) pour se réunir, mais c'est seulement le vélo qui roule et bondit d'une façon rythmée. 🖎 Par le biais des éléments iconographiques, toutes les oeuvres de cette série se soumettent à leur rôle descriptif, illustrant la relation entre l'acte de disposer les composantes du collage, et l'énergie des coups de pinceau.

MEANDRES

🖎 Dans certains de ses collages abstraits Helander reste vague grâce à l'emploi de morceaux de rouleaux imprimés de motifs et d'éléments de décoration. Les lignes font des méandres dans toutes les directions et produisent l'effet linéaire dominant dans ce genre de collage. Ces collages n'offrent pas de répit au spectateur. *Analytical Advice* [pl. 57] met en scène un embrouillamini de lignes blanches et noires, aux caractéristiques cubistes, qui s'agitent dans tous les sens. Dans *Boogy Buff* [pl. 19] les lignes s'élancent d'une carte dans des directions contradictoires. Le «boogy woogy» fait référence aux peintures de Mondrian. Cependant, les méandres des lignes sont en opposition avec l'aspect géométrique de ses peintures. *Jungle Jazz* [pl. 58] est l'un des collages les plus abstraits d'Helander. Il est composé de lettres et de rubans rouges qui tracent une chanson. Le drapeau français ajoute à l'énergie frénétique des boucles des rubans rouges. Au centre, un poulet sans tête court autour d'une ultime icône aux lignes folles et tortueuses. 🖎 Helander se retourne vers un passé qui était symbolisé par les lumières vertes de Gatsby et par la cité d'Emeraude du magicien d'Oz. Les composantes imprégnées de l'âge d'or de l'imprimerie donnent aux collages un aspect à la fois nostalgique et rédempteur. Elles se promènent autour des ombres et jettent des courbes. Cependant, comme dans le meilleur art décoratif, elles retournent irrésistiblement vers la joie de vivre qu'expriment leur mouvement et leur couleur. Avec cette joie, vient l'espoir. Une émotion rare dans cette fin de 20ème siècle, mais qui permet à Bruce Helander de recréer la terre promise.

🖎 Robert Mahoney

*Toutes les citations proviennent d'entretiens avec l'artiste, avril et juillet 1993. **Meyer Schapiro, "The Apples of Cezanne: An essay on the Meaning of Still-life (1968), *Modern Art. 19th and 20th Centuries: Selected Papers* (New York: George Braziller), p. 19.

23. *Torino Tornado*, 1992, collage, 14½ x 11 in. Private Collection, Alpine, NJ

Erotica

24. *Sepia Stance*, 1986, collage, 13 x 10 in. Collection of James Rosenquist, Aripeka, FL

25. *Flower Fire*, 1993, collage, 13 x 9 in. Courtesy of Lorenzo Rodriquez Gallery, Chicago, IL

26. *About Face*, 1983, collage, 10¾ x 7 in. Collection of Kenneth Speiser, Providence, RI

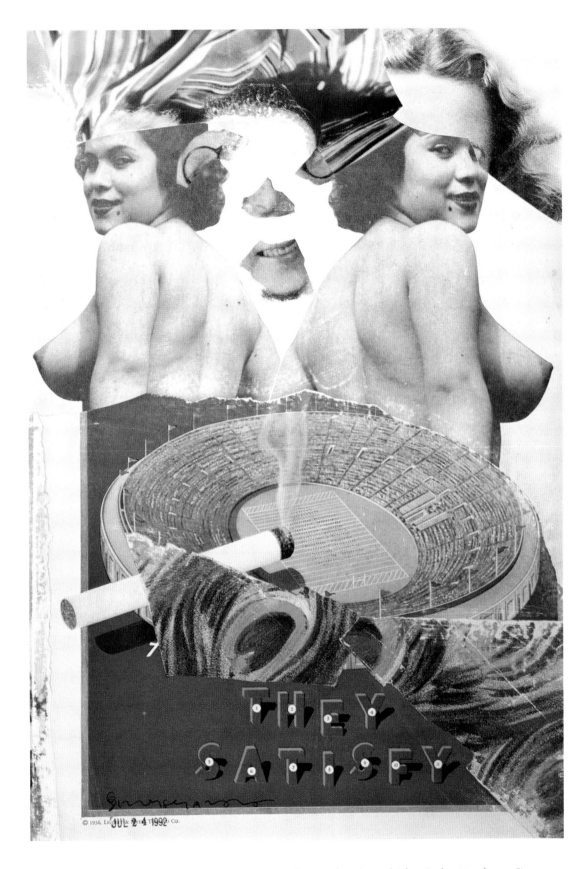

27. *Double Dip*, 1992, collage, 14¾ x 10 in. Collection of T. Alec and Arlette Rigby, Manalapan, FL

28. *Deck Derriere*, 1993, collage, 18 x 11 in. Private Collection, Chicago, IL

29. *Polka Pie*, 1993, collage, 13 x 10 in. Collection of the artist

30. *Record Rendez-vous*, 1993, collage, 11 x 8 in. Courtesy of Galerie Martine-Namy Caulier, Paris, France

Dreams

31. *Heather's Haberdashery*, 1993, collage, 15⅜ x 9½ in. Collection of Richard and Heather Merkin, New York, NY

32. *Mechanic's Meow*, 1993, collage, 9 x 7 in. Private Collection, Hobe Sound, FL

33. *Wonder World*, 1993, collage, 15⅞ x 8½ in. Courtesy of Carl Schlosberg Fine Art, Sherman Oaks, CA

34. *Dream Dame*, 1993, collage, 12 x 8½ in. Courtesy of Marcia Rafelman Fine Arts, Toronto, Canada

35. *Zenith's Zees*, 1993, collage, 10½ x 8½ in. Collection of Zenith Ellis, West Palm Beach, FL

Cartoons

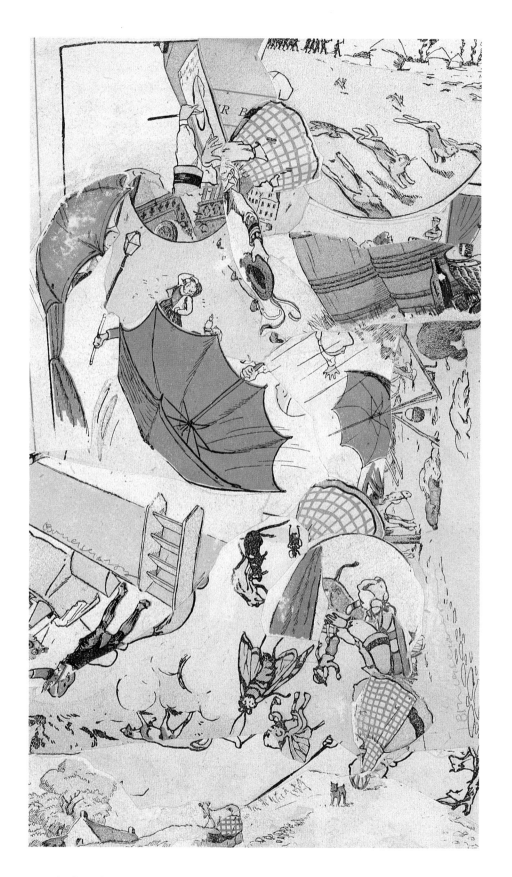

36. *Umbrella Undertow*, 1993, collage, 9 x 5⅜ in. Courtesy of OK Harris Works of Art, New York, NY

37. *Farmhouse Fiasco*, 1993, collage, 8½ x 6½ in. Collection of Krystofer Kimmel, Milan, Italy

38. *Brownie Bonanza*, 1993, collage, 14 x 9½ in. Courtesy of Galerie Martine Namy-Caulier, Paris, France

39. *Beaujolais Bouquet*, 1993, collage, 13 x 9½ in. Collection of Mrs. Arthur Gallant

40. *Star Search*, 1993, collage, 12 x 8½ in. Courtesy of Ron Hall Gallery, Dallas, TX

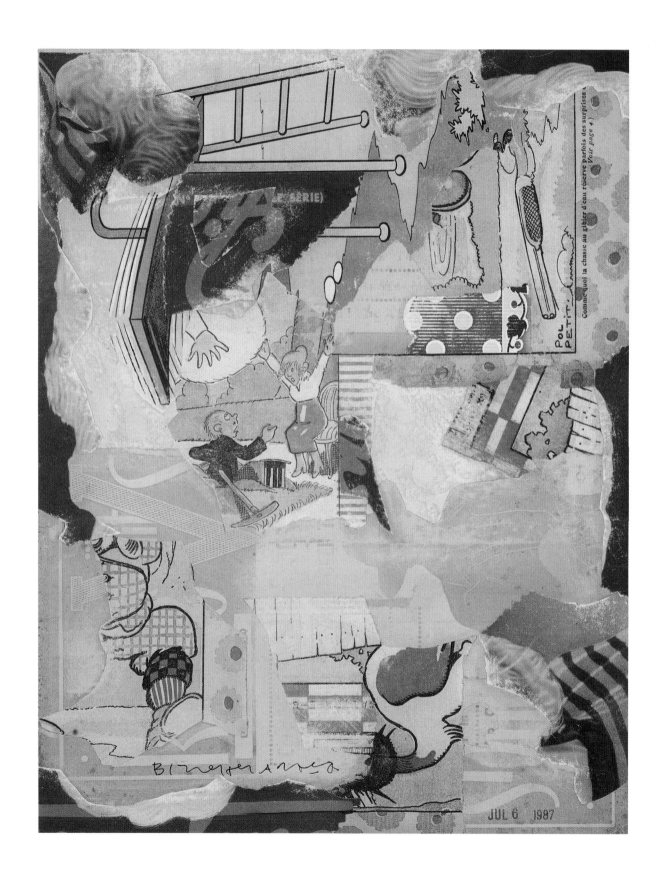

41. *Jumping Jehovahs*, 1987, collage, 16 x 14½ in. Private Collection, Boston, MA

Eccentric Landscapes

42. *Moonlight Monkey*, 1993, collage, 16 x 12½ in. Collection of Alan and Marcia Docter, Telluride, CO

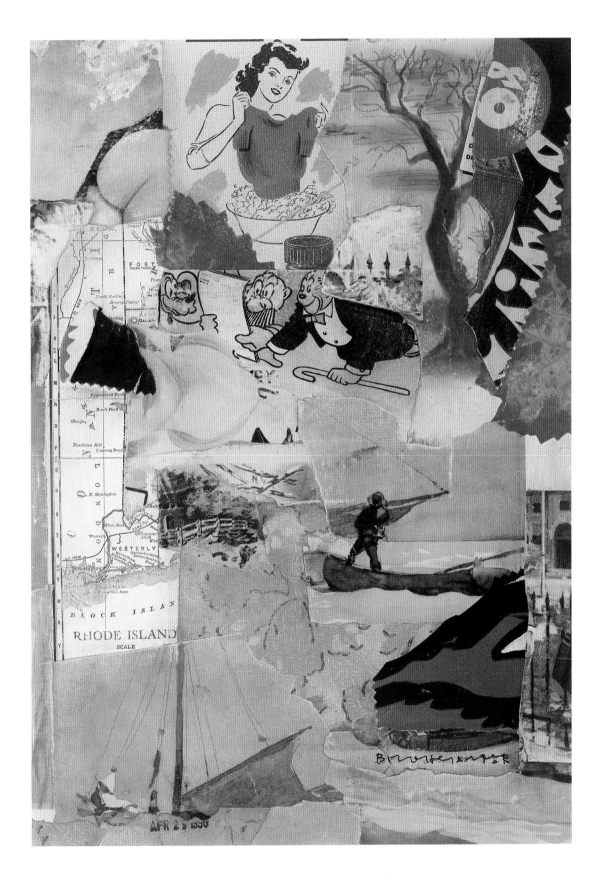

43. *Rhode Island Red*, 1990, collage, 11 x 9½ in. Collection of Dale Chihuly, Seattle, WA

44. *Two Tulips*, 1992, collage, 17 x 21½ in. Collection of Harriet Diamond, West Palm Beach, FL

45. *Private Passage*, 1989, collage, 20 x 15½ in. Collection of Blake Byrne, Los Angeles, CA

46. *Red Routes (Uses for Corn)*, 1993, collage, 14 x 9½ in. Collection of Gitta Kuerten, Dusseldorf, Germany

Painterly Effects

47. *Baby Blues*, 1992, collage, 15 x 9¾ in. Collection of Elizabeth and Michael Rea

48. *Violent Verde*, 1993, collage, 22 x 18½ in. Collection of Larry and Paula Poons, New York, NY

49. *Free Fall*, 1993, collage, 14½ x 11½ in. Courtesy of OK Harris Works of Art, New York, NY

50. *Sophisticated Slide*, 1992, collage, 17¾ x 16 in. Collection of Larry Rivers, New York, NY

51. *Tiptoe Tendency*, 1993, collage, 19 x 14 in. Private Collection

52. *Umbrella Underalls*, 1983, collage, 11 x 9 in. Courtesy of David and Marilyn Friedman, Princeton, NJ

53. *Penguin Plaid*, 1988, collage, 13½ x 10¾ in. Collection of Ashley and Harriet Hoffman, New York, NY

54. *Bubble Bath*, 1987, collage, 25 x 18 in. Courtesy of Eve Mannes Gallery, Atlanta, GA

55. *Outer Orbit*, 1993, collage, 9½ x 7¼ in. Collection of the artist

Meanders

56. *Sugar Swirl*, 1993, collage, 11 x 9 in. Courtesy of Galerie Martine Namy-Caulier, Paris, France

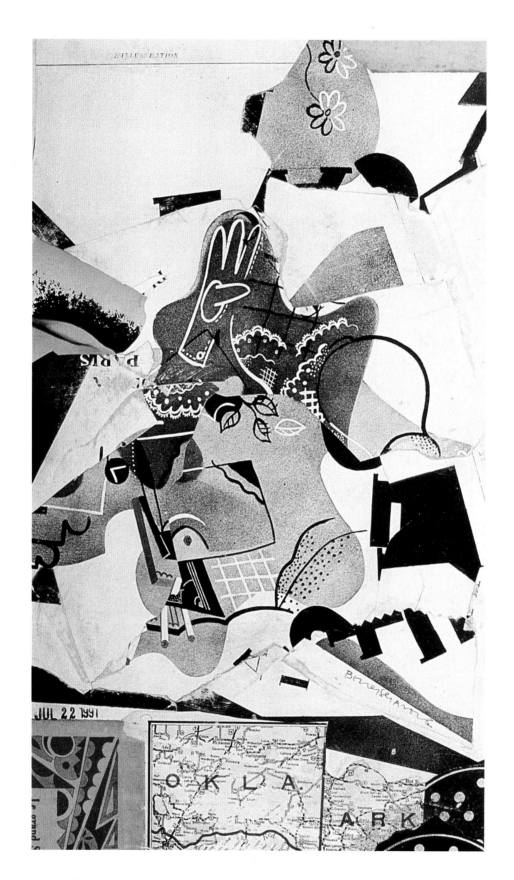

57. *Analytical Advice*, 1991, collage, 15½ x 9 in. Collection of Robert Rauschenberg, Captiva, FL

58. *Jungle Jazz*, 1993, collage, 11½ x 8¾ in. Collection of Marcia and Alan Docter, Telluride, CO

59. *Card Caper*, 1993, collage, 11½ x 9½ in. Courtesy of O.K. Harris Works of Art, New York, NY

60. *Storm Showers*, 1989, silkscreen, 19¾ x 13¼ in. Collection of the Metropolitan Museum of Art, New York, NY

1947   Born in Great Bend, Kansas, to Carmen
        and Amos Helander

1959   Father dies

1963   Mother remarries, family moves to Racine,
        Minnesota

        Attends Midwestern Museum and Art
        Program, University of Kansas, Lawrence,
        Kansas (and in summer 1964)

1965   Graduates high school, enters Rhode Island
        School of Design (RISD), Providence,
        Rhode Island; other classmates include
        Mary Boone, Dale Chihuly, Bill Drew and
        Nicole Miller

1966   Forms rock band called Black River Circus

        Studies with Richard Merkin and Italo Scanga

1968   Begins incorporating collage into illustration
        projects

        Studies photography with Harry Callahan and
        Aaron Siskind and theory with Sewell Sillman

1969   Bachelor of Fine Arts in illustration, RISD

1970   Marries Kathe Mangel

1971   Moves to Washington, D.C., where he is a
        Fellow of the National Endowment for
        the Arts

        Daughter, Klee, is born

1972   Returns to RISD and enrolls in the graduate
        painting program

1973   Appointed Assistant Director of Admissions
        at RISD

        First one-man show in New York,
        Prince Street Gallery

61. Carmen Helander

62. Amos Helander

1975   Appointed Director of Summer Programs,
        Extension Program and
        European Study Seminars at RISD

1976   Accepts position as Associate Provost
        of RISD

1977   Becomes Provost and Vice President of
        Academic Affairs at RISD

1980   Resigns from RISD to develop national art
        magazine, *Art Express*, with offices in
        Providence and New York City

1982   Sells *Art Express*; moves to Palm Beach,
        Florida, to open the Helander Gallery

        Works on collages at night in a former studio
        of Flo Ziegfield and Billy Burke

1986   Included in the exhibition *Collages* with
        Romare Bearden, Buster Cleveland, Joseph
        Cornell and Robert Courtright at New York's
        Forum Gallery; exhibition reviewed by
        Vivien Raynor in *The New York Times*

1987   Travels to Moscow and Leningrad in search
        of collage material

1989   Opens New York branch of Helander Gallery
        in SoHo

        Divorced from Kathe Mangel

1990   One-man exhibition, Carlo Lamagna Gallery,
        New York

1991   Marries Wendy Cohen

1992   Retrospective of collages opens at the Newport
        Art Museum, Newport, Rhode Island; travels
        to The Butler Institute of American Art,
        Youngstown, Ohio and Wake Forest
        University Fine Arts Gallery, Winston-Salem,
        North Carolina

        First one-man exhibition in Paris Galerie
        Martine Namy-Caulier

        Cast in bronze by Duane Hanson for sculp-
        ture titled *The Art Dealer*

1993   Interviewed for *Good Day Chicago*, Fox
        Television, in conjunction with his one-man
        exhibition at Chicago's Lorenzo Rodriguez
        Gallery

        Divorced from Wendy Cohen
        Commissioned to design poster for Palm
        Beach International Film Festival

        Commissioned by *The New Yorker* for collage
        illustration for the December 20 issue

        Appointed to the Architectural Review Board,
        Palm Beach, FL

63. *Si, Si Senor*, 1972, assemblage, 60 x 120 in.
Graduate M.F.A. exhibition, Rhode Island School of Design, Providence, RI

Collections & Exhibitions

Public Collections

Albany Museum of Art, Albany, GA
Boca Raton Museum of Art, Boca Raton, FL
Boyar Corporation, New York, NY
Butler Art Institute, Youngstown, OH
Center for the Arts, Vero Beach, FL
Charles A. Wustum Museum, Racine, WI
Cranbrook Academy, Bloomfield Hills, MI
Danville Museum of Fine Arts, Danville, VA
Grand Rapids Art Museum, Grand Rapids, MI
Hudson River Museum, Yonkers, NY
Kemper Museum of Art and Design, Kansas City, MO
Metropolitan Museum of Art, New York, NY
Milwaukee Art Museum, Milwaukee, WI
Museum of Art, Fort Lauderdale, FL
Newport Art Museum, Newport, RI
Norton Gallery of Art, West Palm Beach, FL
Philadelphia Museum of Art, Philadelphia, PA
Portland Art Museum, Portland, OR
Rochester Municipal Airport, Rochester, MN
Smithsonian Institution, Washington, D. C.
Spencer Museum of Art, Lawrence, KS
Textron Corporation, Providence, RI
The Art Institute of Chicago, Chicago, IL
Union County College Museum of Art, Union, NJ
Wellesley College Museum, Wellesley, MA

Selected One-Man Exhibitions

1994   OK Harris Works of Art, Detroit, MI
        Arij Gasiunasen Fine Arts, Palm Beach, FL
        Arden Gallery, Boston, MA
        Marcia Rafelman Fine Arts, Toronto, Ontario, Canada
        Carl Schlosberg Fine Arts, Sherman Oaks, CA
        Jeanine Cox Fine Art, Miami Beach, FL
1993   Lorenzo Rodriguez Gallery, Chicago, IL
        Galerie Martine Namy-Caulier, Paris, France
        Butler Institute of American Art, Youngstown, OH

Carl Schlosberg Fine Arts, Sherman Oaks, CA
OK Harris Works of Art, Birmingham, MI
1992   Newport Art Museum, Newport, RI (Retrospective, Collages 1969-1992)
        Galerie Martine Namy-Caulier, Paris, France
        Wake Forest University Museum, Winston-Salem, NC
        Virginia Beach Center for the Arts, Virginia Beach, VA
1991   OK Harris Works of Art, Birmingham, MI
1990   Virginia Lynch Gallery, Tiverton, RI
        Carlo Lamagna Gallery, New York, NY
1988   Shippee Gallery, New York, NY
1987   J. P. Natkin Gallery, New York, NY
        Kastoriano-Shoshan Gallery, New York, NY
        Tilghman Gallery, Boca Raton, FL
1977   Watson Gallery, Wheaton College, Norton, MA
1976   Smith College, Northhampton, MA
        Moore College of Art, Philadelphia, PA
        Warren Gallery, Warren, RI
1975   Palazzo Cenci, Rome, Italy
        What Cheer Arts Gallery, Providence, RI
1973   Loeb Art Center, Harvard University, Cambridge, MA
        Prince Street Gallery, New York, NY
1972   Loomis Gallery, Windsor, CT
1970   Woods-Gerry Gallery, Providence, RI

Selected Group Exhibitions

1994   OK Harris Works of Art, New York, NY
        Ron Hall Gallery, Dallas, TX
        Marcia Rafelman Fine Arts, Toronto, Ontario, Canada
1993   Vero Beach Center for the Arts, "Collage & Assemblage," Vero Beach, FL
        OK Harris Works of Art, New York, NY
        Virginia Lynch Gallery, Tiverton, RI
        Philharmonic Center for the Arts, "Greetings From Florida," Naples, FL
1992   Museum of Art, "Stars in Florida," curated by David Miller, Fort Lauderdale, FL

1991   OK Harris Works of Art, "Centennial Biennial Invitational," New York, NY
        Carl Schlosberg Fine Arts, Sherman Oaks, CA
        Gallery des Artistes, "A Gathering of South Florida Artists," West Palm Beach, FL
        Ruth Siegel Gallery, New York, NY

1989   OK Harris South, "New Work-New York," Miami, FL
        Shippee Gallery, "75th Anniversary — Art at the Armory Show," New York, NY

1988   Artifacts, "Fourth Anniversary Exhibition," Miami, FL
        Littlejohn-Smith Gallery, New York
        Artifacts, "Small Works," Miami, FL

1987   Joy Moos Gallery, "Tribute to Andy Warhol," Miami, FL
        Boca Raton Museum of Art, "36th All Florida Annual," Boca Raton, FL (Juror: Lowrey Sims, Assistant Curator, Metropolitan Museum of Art)
        NOW Gallery, "East Village Micro Show," New York, NY
        Frank Bernarducci Gallery, Summer Exhibition, New York, NY
        J. P. Natkin Gallery, New York, NY
        Artifacts Art Salon, Miami, FL
        Shippee Gallery, "Poetic License," New York, NY
        OK Harris South, "Florida Invitational," Miami, FL
        Viridian Gallery, La Jolla, CA
        The Flagler Museum, "Mitzi Newhouse Art Preview," Palm Beach, FL

1986   Diane Brown Gallery, "RISD in New York," New York, NY
        Forum Gallery, "Collages," New York, NY
        Museum of Art, "28th Hortt Memorial," Fort Lauderdale, FL
        NOW Gallery, "Micro," New York, NY
        OK Harris South, "Inaugural Show," Miami, FL
        Littlejohn-Smith Gallery, "Dog Days of Summer," curated by Fred Boyle, O. K. Harris, New York, NY
        Nancy Hoffman Gallery, New York, NY

1985   Society of the Four Arts, "47th Annual Exhibition of Contemporary American Paintings," Palm Beach, FL (Juror: James Demetrion, Director, Hirshhorn Museum, Washington, D.C.)
        Zimmerman Saturn Gallery, "Inaugural Show," Nashville, TN

1984   Rollins College, "The Face in the Mirror," Artine Artinian Collection, Self-Portraits by Florida Artists, Winter Park, FL
        Hirondelle Gallery, New York, NY
        Norton Gallery of Art, West Palm Beach, FL

1982   The Lily Iselin Gallery, Providence, RI

1981   The Lily Iselin Gallery, Providence, RI

1979   Brown University, List Art Gallery, Providence, RI

1978   Temple University, Tyler School of Art, Philadelphia, PA

1977   RISD, "Space Window," Woods-Gerry Gallery, Providence, RI

1976   University of Manitoba, School of Art, Winnipeg, Canada
        Hudson D. Walker Gallery, Provincetown, MA
        Brown University, List Art Gallery, Providence, RI

1975   Roger Williams Park, Visiting Artist, "FATAGAGA," Providence, RI
        Art Park, Artist-in-Residence, Lewiston, NY
        Provincetown Art Association, Provincetown, MA

1974   Woods-Gerry Gallery, Two-Man Show, (William Drew), Providence, RI
        Browne Art Gallery, Western Illinois University, Macomb, IL

1973   International Correspondence Exhibition, Miniham Gallery, Depere, WI

1971   15th National Exhibition, Fall River Art Association, Fall River, MA
        Botolph Gallery, Cambridge, MA

1970   Newport Art Association, Juried Painting Show, Newport, RI, 1970
        Bi-Annual Faculty Exhibition, Museum of Art, RISD, Providence, RI, also 1972, 1974, 1976, 1978

Bibliography

Adler, Jane. "Helander's Art: It's not a Put-on," *Providence Sunday Journal Arts and Leisure*, November 3, 1974, p. H-ll.

Allen, Jane. Magazine Review (includes "Best Reading"), *New Art Examiner*, January, 1982, p. 5.

Alloway, Lawrence. "Art Mediation," *Village Voice*, October 7, 1982, p. 4.

Boynton, Andrew. "Openings," *Art & Antiques*, June 1988, p. 31.

Collins, Amy Fine. "Bruce Helander at Shippee Gallery," *Art in America*, January 1989, p. 152-3.

DiLauro, Stephen. "Curious Collage," *Downtown*, October 14, 1987, p. 21-A.

Dougherty, Philip II. "Media Reports," *WQXR, The New York Times*, April 28, 1981.

Engel, Mary. "Artscape: Changes in the Art Market," *Miami Review*, March 13, 1992.

Fitzgerald, John R. "R.I.S.D.'s Hall Cites Major Moves, Key Appointment," *Providence Journal*, February 19, 1979, p. 14.

Genz, Michelle. "Lecturer Sees Art Lane on Roadsides: Center Talk Focuses on Good, Bad and Ugly," *Miami Herald*, January 31, 1986, p. lPB.

Grove, Nancy. "In the Galleries," *Art & Antiques*, May 1990, p. 151.

Graboys, Lois. "Helander's Recent Work," *Providence Sunday Journal*, February 1968, p. 14D.

Guthrie, Derek. "Media Coups," *New Art Examiner*, September 1981, p. 46.

Hall, Susan. "Down Palm Beach Way," *South Florida*, September 1993, pp. 74-77.

Hieronymous, Clara. "Works on Paper at Zimmerman Saturn Gallery," *The Tennessean*, January 8, 1986, p. D-1.

Hurlburt, Roger. "Talent Shines With Stars of Florida," *Sun-Sentinel*, February 16, 1992.

Isaacson, Philip. "OUTRAGEOUS! — A critic's view of the All-Maine Biennial," *Maine Sunday Telegram*, August 2, 1981, p. 6D.

Koller, Helmut. "Nackte im Fenster," *Style*, May 1988, p. 62.

Kohen, Helen. "Stars in Florida Shines on Transplanted Artists," *Miami Herald*, February 23, 1992.

Lynne, Jill. "Palm Beach Access," June 1986, pp. 30-41.

Mahoney, Robert. "Bruce Helander at J. P. Natkin Gallery," *Arts Magazine*, December, 1987.

Marcus, David. "Art in Palm Beach," *Miami Herald*, Monday, March 28, 1983, pp. lA, 7A.

Marx, Linda. "The Art of the Dealer," *Palm Beach Life*, February 1992, pp. 16-18.

Marzorati, Gerald. "Checking out the Express Line," *SoHo Weekly News*, April 1-7, 1981, p. 23.

— "Push comes to shove at Art Express," *SoHo Weekly News*, June 24, 1981, p. 48.

Milinaire, Catherine. "Best Bets — For Art's Sake," *New York Magazine*, June 1, 1981, p. 4.

Morrison, Lisa. "Helander's Collages," *Art Train*, *WJAR-TV*, March 1978.

Orr, John. "Thinking Abstract: 'Art From Two Continents'," *The Palm Beacher*, February 27, 1986, p. 20.

Perl, Jed. "Successes," *New Criterion*, May 1990, pp. 54-55.

Pantalone, John. "Expressly Providence," *East Side-West Side*, April 16, 1981, p. 48.

Raynor, Vivien. "Contemporary Collages," *The New York Times*, December 19, 1986.

Rubin, Ed. "The Dog Days of August," *New Art Examiner*, November 1986, p. 56.

Schwan, Gary, "Florida Artists Shine at Exhibit," *Palm Beach Post*, February 21, 1992.

— "Norton Artists' Guild Show Review," *Palm Beach Post*, December 18, 1983.

— "Four Arts Competition is an Annual Exercise in Humility," *Palm Beach Post*, December 5, 1985, p B1.

— "First-Rate 'Tie-Ins' Good Supplement to Museum Show," February 14, 1986, p. E7.

— "Juried Show Sleek, Diverse," *Palm Beach Post*, August 28, 1988, p. 2L.

Suprynowica, Vin. "Taking On New York," *The Providence Eagle*, May 21, 1981, p. 1.

Turner, Elisa. "At the Galleries — OK South," *Miami Herald*, July 15, 1988, p. 2W.

Wedekind, Beate. "Mein Rendezvous," *Bunte magazine*, May / June 1984, p. 182.

Wolff, Millie. "Helander Gallery Brings SoHo to Palm Beach," *Palm Beach Daily News*, March 27, 1985,
p. 5.

Yolles, Sandra. "Bruce Helander Collages at OK Harris," *ARTnews*, March 1992, p. 140.

— "Fatagaga, Festival Art - Conceptual & Actual," *National Endowment for the Arts Newsletter*, October 1979, p. 8.

— "Media Notes From All Over," *New York Magazine*, June 23, 1981, p. 28.

— "Through the Artist's Work: Lieberman sculpture-Helander Dedication," *Palm Beach Post*, January 18, 1986, p. 1.

— "Signs of Intelligent Life," *Downtown*, October 22, 1986, p. 3-A.

— "ARTnews Anniversary — Vasari Diary," *ARTnews*, December 1988.

— "Style Statements," *Palm Beach Life*, April, 1992, pp. 36-41.

Articles by the Artist

"Udvardy pulls off artistic stick-up," *New Bedford Times*, February 28-March 1, 1979, p. 2.

"Last Look," *Art Express*, May-June 1981, p. 96.

"Between the Covers," *Art Express*, September-October, 1981, p. 7.

"Camouflage as Art," *Art Express*, November-December 1981, p. 7.

"Who's Who, Who's Where, What's What," *Art Express*, January-February 1982, pp. 14-16.

"April Gornick Paints," *Art Express*, January-February 1982, p. 50.

"Art Outdoors," *Art Express*, January-February 1982, p. 79.

"Art City Motel," *Art Express*, May-June 1982, p. 82.

"Exhibition Review," Peter Voulkos, Thomas Segal Gallery, *Art Express*, September-October 1982, p. 59.

"Ben's Dream" (art book review), *Art Express*, May-June 1982, p. 24.

"The Nelson A. Rockefeller Collection, Masterpieces of Modern Art" (art book review), *Art Express*, May-June 1982, p. 23.

"Roadside Architecture," *Art Express*, May-June, 1982, p. 44.

"Vanishing Roadside America" (art book review), *Art Express*, May-June 1982, p. 24.

"Matisse: Fifty Years of His Graphic Art" (art book review), *Art Express*, May-June 1982, p. 22.

"Wolf Kahn, Landscape Painter" (art book review), *Art Express*, May-June 1982, p. 24.

"Public Art Lift-Off, The Lannan Collection and Public Sculpture," *ARTS Magazine* (Palm Beach County Council of the Arts), February-March 1986, p. 10.

Foreword, "The Real Thing," exhibition catalogue, North Miami Museum, 1985.

Notes

Colophon

EDITOR
Bonnie Clearwater

COPY EDITOR
Sue Henger

RESEARCHERS
Susan Hall and Kimberly Marrero

TRANSLATOR
Katell Besnard

PHOTOGRAPHERS
Robert Nelson
Michael Price

DESIGNER
Elaine Weber

First printing
1,000 copies cloth
1,000 copies paperback

Published by Grassfield Press
Printed and bound in Hong Kong

64. *Time Traveller*, collage, 28 x 16 in. Originally in *The New Yorker* ©1993. All rights reserved.